D1643576

The Kindness Pact

Domonique Bertolucci

hardie grant books

MELBOURNE · LONDON

Published in 2014 by Hardie Grant Books

Hardie Grant Books (Australia)
Ground Floor, Building 1
658 Church Street
Richmond, Victoria 3121
www.hardiegrant.com.au

Hardie Grant Books (UK)
5th & 6th Floor
52–54 Southwark Street
London SE1 1RU
www.hardiegrant.co.uk

A Cataloguing-in-Publication entry is available from the catalogue of
the National Library of Australia at www.nla.gov.au

The Kindness Pact
ISBN 978 1 74270 859 1

Cover design by Kinart
Typeset in Plantin Light 10.75/16 pt by Cannon Typesetting
Printed and bound in China by 1010 Printing International Limited

For Sophia and Tobias

Contents

You yourself,
as much as anybody in the entire universe,
deserve your love and affection.

Gautama Buddha

Preface

Have you ever wondered why some people seem to breeze through life, enjoying themselves and taking everything in their stride, and yet others spend all their time worrying about this and agonising over that? Why does self-confidence come so easily to some people? And how can you make sure it comes easily to you?

Confidence comes from within.

So many people are looking outside themselves for ways to feel good on the inside. They think self-confidence will come from doing this, having that or looking a certain way. The reality is, although they are the only person who can build their confidence up, the way they think and act is doing nothing but tearing it down.

The first seeds for this book were planted a few years ago when I was walking in the park and observed a scene that left me feeling quite uncomfortable. A young boy of perhaps six or seven had climbed a tree and gone beyond the height he was confident to get back down from. I couldn't help but overhear his mother berate him for his lack of courage. 'Don't be so pathetic.' 'You really are being stupid.' 'What a wimp you're being.' 'You really are useless.' On and on she went as the little boy cried in fear and humiliation. Eventually, much to my relief, a companion stepped in and helped this little boy down from the tree, his self-confidence destroyed and belief in his tree-climbing potential in tatters.

I felt ill at both the words I'd heard and the hostility with which they were spoken, and I couldn't begin to imagine the impact they'd had on the person they had been directed at. At the same time the words this mother spoke had an unpleasant familiarity to them because, while most people would agree this woman had handled the situation with her son badly and recognise that the way she spoke is no way to get the best out of a child, the words she used were the very same words I had heard countless people, both in my professional and personal life, use to berate or belittle their own efforts.

When you interact with a child, you are, in that moment, the guardian of their self-esteem. But as an adult, you are the guardian of your own. No-one can nurture and protect your confidence and self-belief except you.

You are the guardian of your self-esteem.
Guard it vigilantly.

Introducing the Eight Promises

It's been many years since I wrote my first book, *Your Best Life: The ultimate guide to creating the life you want*. While I'm still very proud of it and think it's the perfect guide to getting what you want from life, over the years I've realised that there is something just as important as, if not more important than, achieving your goals: feeling good about yourself regardless.

Feeling good about who you are and the life you live shouldn't depend on a specific outcome, yet all too often I hear people put themselves down or beat themselves up because they haven't done this or got that. Your confidence shouldn't be dependent on the goals you have achieved, nor should it be dependent on the feedback you get from others, your dress size or the amount in your bank account.

Building and maintaining your confidence and self-worth is something that has to come from within and yet the truth is, most people are terribly unkind to themselves. They make harsh judgements, engage in endless self-criticism and are unforgiving of even the smallest of failings … and then wonder why they don't feel so great about themselves.

At the same time these people are often loving and kind parents, generous and encouraging friends, and supportive and committed colleagues. They give everyone else their best, only to give themselves their worst.

When I share this observation with people, the first thing they invariably try to do is explain why their self-criticism or negative self-talk is valid. Catching themselves in this act of *confidence sabotage*, the penny slowly drops.

But if your self-confidence isn't based on what you've got or what you've done, how do you build and maintain it?

The answer is deceptively simple. Make the commitment to treat yourself with the same kindness you show the other important people in your life.

The key to feeling good about who you are and the life you live is built on this pact – the **Eight Promises**. Each chapter of this book represents a different promise and explains the role it plays in building and maintaining your confidence and self-belief.

The First Promise: Accept your imperfections

I am perfectly imperfect.

There is no such thing as perfection and yet so many people exhaust themselves and erode their confidence in the pursuit of it. When you accept your imperfections, you recognise you have strengths and weaknesses. You acknowledge that, like everyone else, you have many positive qualities but that you also have other, less positive ones … and that's okay.

Once you have released yourself from the burden of perfectionism and accepted your imperfections, you are free to use your positive qualities to their fullest. You can also decide which of your less-than-ideal qualities you would like to invest your energy in improving and which qualities everyone else will need to accept as 'part of the parcel'.

The Second Promise: Always do your best

I always do my best and my best is always good enough.

When you set impossible goals that you have no real chance of achieving, you are setting yourself up for

failure; when you promise to always do your best you
are able to have much more realistic expectations of
yourself and what you can achieve. Your sense of self-
worth will no longer be dependent on outcomes and
you will feel good about who you are regardless of
what you have or haven't been able to achieve.

When you truly believe your best is good enough,
you can accept that you are having a bad day, or
feeling a bit ordinary, without this affecting the way
you feel about yourself.

The Third Promise: Stop comparing yourself

*I have no need to see myself as more or less than
anyone else.*

Whether it's your neighbours, celebrities or the people
that you see on reality TV, comparing yourself to
others will usually leave you feeling inadequate. Even
if you find yourself thinking that you are better or
superior in some way, this will only give your self-
esteem a short-term boost.

When you stop comparing yourself to others, the
only person you will need to impress is yourself. You
will be able to source your confidence from within

and it will no longer be affected by anything anyone else says, does or has.

The Fourth Promise: Believe in your potential

I fully expect my life to be happy and rewarding.
Not only is worrying a big waste of energy, it also sends a clear message to your subconscious about your expectations in life. Instead of worrying about things that might never happen, when you believe in your potential, you are able to focus your attention and your efforts on making the things you do want your reality.

You don't have to be in denial about negative things that could happen, but once you've acknowledged your fears or the worst-case scenario, you are able to put them to the side and continue on towards the happy and rewarding future you know you deserve.

The Fifth Promise: Silence your inner critic

I only welcome thoughts that support and encourage me.
Think of yourself as the guardian of your self-esteem. The way you speak to yourself has a big bearing on how you feel about yourself; if you speak to yourself in a harsh, critical or belittling way, your confidence

will wither, but if you silence your inner critic and never speak to yourself more harshly than you would to a small child, you will nurture your confidence and allow your self-esteem to flourish.

Changing the way you think takes practice, but while initially you might not be able to control every single thought you have, you will always be able to decide which ones you want to pay attention to.

The Sixth Promise: Challenge yourself

I am brave and willing to step outside of my comfort zone.

Confidence and self-belief are like muscles; you need to exercise them if you want them to grow stronger. One of the best ways to build these muscles is by stepping outside of your comfort zone. When you challenge yourself, you are telling your subconscious that you believe in yourself and that you are willing to back yourself in new circumstances and situations. Regardless of how you feel while doing something new, you will always feel great for having done it.

When you step outside of your comfort zone, take on a challenge or learn something new, you open yourself up to the added confidence boost

of discovering that you are actually not so bad at
something you never knew you could do.

The Seventh Promise: Stop making excuses

I take full responsibility for who I am and the life I lead.
Regardless of how it may look from afar, nobody is
living the perfect life. What some people are better at
than others is living their best life. If you are not living
your best life, you need to examine not only the things
that are getting in your way, but the reasons why you
are letting them.

When you stop making excuses and start taking
responsibility you are able to enjoy the things that are
great about your life, while harbouring no illusions
about what you need to change if you are to enjoy
everything else.

The Eighth Promise: Love yourself

I always treat myself with love and respect.
If you want to feel good about who you are and
the life you live, you need to make building your
confidence and your self-belief a high priority.

Love yourself. Treat yourself with as much
love and respect as you would your closest friend,

be understanding and forgiving of your failings and, above all, be as kind to yourself as you are to the other important people in your life.

When you commit to the **Eight Promises**, your life you will no longer be burdened with anxiety, doubt or insecurity and instead you will feel good about who you are and the life you live. Not just some of the time, but all of the time.

If you would like to learn even more about the **Eight Promises** and how to change the way you feel about who you are and the life you live, you can download *The Kindness Pact Workbook*, full of exercises, ideas and inspiration, free from domoniquebertolucci.com.

Accept your imperfections

I am perfectly imperfect.

You are good enough.

Feeling good about who you are and the life you live begins with your acceptance of yourself. You don't need to wait until you are perfect; you are good enough just as you are.

As you read that statement, how did you respond? Did you start making excuses for why it couldn't possibly be true? Did you immediately launch into a list of reasons why you're not good enough and things you need to change about yourself, improve or work on?

For so many people, the desire to be perfect is so ingrained that they don't even realise it is something they are pursuing. For others, being perfect or the acute recognition of exactly how far they are from this desired state fills their every waking moment with disappointment and frustration in themselves.

Perfection is an unachievable goal. Nobody can be perfect … not even you.

Breaking out of this cycle of confidence sabotage requires a new way of thinking – a way of thinking that leads to a healthier, confidence-enhancing relationship with yourself. When you embrace the Kindness Pact, you make the commitment to treat yourself with the same kindness, compassion and respect as you do the other important people in your life. Do you expect your friends, your partner, your boss, your colleagues, your children or your parents to be perfect? I doubt it very much. Of course they will have flaws that will annoy you, frustrate you or downright drive you insane, but for the most part, consciously or subconsciously, you will have accepted this as a part of who they are.

When my husband and I first began living together, which seems like forever ago, I noticed at the end of each day he would relax on the sofa and take off his socks … and leave them there! If I didn't pick them up, by the end of the week, there would be seven pairs of socks piled up by the side of the sofa. I wish I was exaggerating, but I'm not. Now, my husband is a modern man; he doesn't expect me to wait on him hand and foot, he doesn't wreak havoc wherever he goes – he's actually generally tidy. He's a hands-on-dad, nappies have never scared him and he is the perfect partner in so many things … except when it comes to socks.

Now, most people who are reading this (except for the true neat-freaks amongst you) are probably thinking something along the lines of, 'Yeah, but it's just a couple of pairs of socks; he sounds like a pretty good catch to me.' My thoughts exactly. And exactly my point. We don't expect the people in our lives to be perfect. As intelligent adults, we know it is unreasonable to expect the people in our lives to be perfect. As frustrating as it can sometimes be, we know the people in our lives will have a whole range of qualities: some we like, a few we really don't like and many that we are indifferent about.

Like it or not, we know we have to accept these flaws as 'part of the whole package'. Some things are easier to accept – I'm sure I'll be telling the story about the socks at our 50th wedding anniversary – and others are much tougher. But, except for truly heinous character flaws, accept them we know we must.

It is no less unreasonable to expect yourself to be perfect than it is to expect perfection from the people you love.

And yet so rarely do people offer themselves the same generosity. In my work, and for that matter my day-to-day conversations, I hear people beat themselves up over all manner of things, often

directing the same ferocity to ordinary stu.
and minor foibles as they do major mistakes, a.
with no sign of the kindness and acceptance they
would show the other people they value in their lives.
It is unreasonable to expect the people you love to
be perfect and it is equally unreasonable to expect
perfection of yourself.

If you want to feel good about yourself and
develop the kind of self-esteem that is robust enough
to withstand the challenges that may be thrown at you
in life, you need to recognise many of the things you
perceive as flaws as an intrinsic part of who you are.

Learn to accept your flaws
with love and grace.

If one of your closest friends was asked to describe
you, do you know what they would they say? If they
were feeling particularly honest, they might include
one or two of your flaws, but by and large their

s on your positive qualities and
ve chosen to be your friend.
asked to describe one of your
ure you would respond in much

Treat ⅄ your own best friend. Nurture
and protect your self-esteem by focussing on your
positive qualities and accepting that, while you might
have a few less-than-positive ones, these really are a
'part of the parcel' of being you.

You are good enough just as you are. Your
confidence and self-belief are dependent on your
acceptance of this statement as fact. This isn't just
true for some people; it's true for everyone. Gwyneth
Paltrow, Academy Award–winning actress and founder
of the popular website GOOP.com, admitted to *InStyle*
that accepting herself as she is, and for who she is, is
something she is still learning how to do: 'I'm hard on
myself, so I'm working on shifting perspective toward
self-acceptance, with all my flaws and weaknesses.'

The very concept of self-acceptance can be an
overwhelming idea for so many people. As you read
this statement, many thoughts and feelings may be
presenting themselves to you. You might be thinking,

'If I'm not perfect, then what will I be?' 'If there is nothing wrong with me, then why is my life not perfect?'

But the reason your life isn't perfect is because there is no such thing as 'perfect'. Perfectionism is an unachievable goal. Nobody can be perfect … not even you.

You are good enough just as you are.

Finally coming to this realisation and accepting that you will never be perfect can be an incredibly liberating experience.

The quest for perfection is a lost cause. It's entirely subjective and completely unachievable. You don't need to be perfect to be a good person. The *you* that you are right now is good enough.

When you are a motivated person, someone who likes to do things well or who has ambitions for their life, it's easy to think that not only do you have to give 150 per cent effort, you need to give *everything* 150 per cent effort. You don't.

If you try to be perfect at everything you do, not only will you fail, you'll be placing yourself under enormous pressure and stress. And to what end? So you can be brilliant at things that, when it comes down to it, don't really even matter to you?

Perfectionism and self-confidence cannot coexist.

Of course there are some things that it is important you excel at. For me, this list includes things like the kind of parent I am to my children and partner I am to my husband; the kind of environment I create for my family; and the quality of support I provide as a friend. It's very important that I do a great job at sharing my thoughts and ideas in things like this book and in the programs and courses I run at domoniquebertolucci. com. I don't need to be perfect at these things, but I really do want to do them brilliantly.

But these are not the only things I do with my time. Like most people, if I let myself, I can be pulled into a million different directions at once, asked to participate in one hundred and one different initiatives and be drowned by admin, paperwork and the other minutiae of day-to-day life. The difference is, I know I don't need to be perfect at all of these things. The honest truth is that for most of it, it doesn't even matter if I'm particularly good. I'm not saying I'm careless, sloppy or slapdash. Simply that I choose a few things that I want to excel at and accept that I may never be more than average at the rest.

Decide what you want to be brilliant at and be okay with just being okay at the rest.

The list above is just my list and yours may be entirely different. You may want to excel at your career, enjoy peak fitness and have the most stylish and stunning wardrobe. Or it could be that you choose to focus on your family, your community and your garden and can happily let the rest take care of itself. The important thing to remember is that you don't have to be perfect at anything, let alone try to be perfect at everything.

Instead of judging yourself for what you can or can't do, appreciate the commitment you make and the effort you take with the things that are important to you.

Some people pursue perfection – the perfect job, perfect relationship, perfect home or perfect body – in the hope that it will make them feel good about themselves; make them happy. In fact, the opposite is true. For as long as you try to be perfect, you will always fall short of your expectations. Whenever you feel that you have been less than you could have been, no matter how unrealistic those expectations might have been, you create an emotional experience where you feel inadequate, inferior or *less than*, a state that actively erodes your confidence and self-esteem.

My client Susan had spent her whole life trying to be perfect, whether it was getting top grades when she was a student, earning accolades at work or getting back into her size-eight jeans after her children were born. Susan had all but exhausted herself trying to do it all, be it all and have it all.

Perfectionism is the enemy of happiness.

As the years passed it became harder and harder to maintain this veneer of perfection. With 5.30 am gym workouts and midnight bake-sale cooking sessions, it was clear to everyone around her that she was heading for a serious case of burnout. I expressed my concerns to Susan, but she wasn't ready to listen.

Seeking perfection is a vicious cycle. You don't believe you are good enough as you are, so you try to be perfect. Perfection is impossible to achieve, so you fail to do or be all that you set out to be. Having failed, you don't feel so good about yourself and on the downward spiral goes.

Susan's exhaustion finally caught up with her. She found herself in bed for a week with a nasty case of pneumonia. She began the week feeling anxious, emotional and seriously stressed out, but as it progressed she found herself relaxing and actually enjoying the fact that her doctor had ordered her to do nothing.

From her new calm perspective, Susan could see that her children had been fed and homework had been done. Her colleagues had pitched in and her workload had been shared around. Rodents hadn't taken over her home. Sure, her daughter hadn't gone to school with perfect braids and her son had attended football training with mismatched socks. The report she had been working on hadn't included all the information she would've included. But even from her sickbed, Susan could see that these things didn't really matter … not in the greater scheme of things.

The person you are, right here, right now, flaws and all is a worthwhile, valuable and valid human being.

Returning to work with a promise to her doctor to take it easy, Susan made another promise, this time to herself. From now on, she was going to give her best efforts to the things that really mattered and was no longer going to exhaust herself trying to be perfect at the rest.

The easiest way to escape the debilitating nature of perfectionism is to remind yourself that *you are good enough.*

No-one is saying that there aren't things you could improve or that your character is flawless. But if you never become a better person than you are today – thinner, richer, healthier, smarter, more committed, more efficient, more dedicated, less impatient, less stubborn – if none of this ever changes, you will still be just fine as you are.

This doesn't mean that there isn't room for improvement or that you can't continue to grow and develop as a person; simply that the person you are today is good enough. You. Are. Good. Enough.

This can be hard to remember. We live in a society where we are bombarded by messages and images from the media designed precisely to make us feel like we are *less than* or not good enough in some way, in their attempt to make us think if we just got some of whatever it is they are selling our lives would be better and we would be one very significant step closer to our holy grail of perfection.

Listen to your inner dialogue and you will be surprised how many times you find you are either trying to be perfect or apologising because you're not. It is so unnecessary. You don't criticise your friends and loved ones for failing to meet some idealistic version of perfection, so why should you criticise yourself in that way?

*Don't apologise for who you are
or criticise yourself for who you are not.*

There is a big difference between accepting your imperfections and not wanting to improve yourself or grow as a person. I am a passionate believer in lifelong learning, and a part of my quest is to continually discover how to be a better version of myself, whether that means expanding my knowledge and learning new things, taking on a new physical challenge or getting a better understanding of my thoughts and my feelings so I can have even better-quality relationships.

I wholeheartedly encourage the desire to improve and grow, but it must come from a healthy place, where you recognise all your positive qualities and seek to develop as a person, not one where you make a huge list of all the ways you fall short and then systematically try to perfect yourself.

You are not broken
and you do not need to be fixed.

In my work as a coach I've seen so many people take low self-esteem and perfectionism and dress it up as an interest in self-help and personal improvement. You are not helping yourself if you use this information to make yourself feel bad or as if you are lost, failing or inadequate in some way. The thirst for knowledge is a wonderful thing. Quench yours, but be clear about what you are drinking and why.

Some sceptics might scoff that here I am, a 'self-help' author myself, writing about not becoming addicted to self-help. But, as an alcohol manufacturer must put a 'drink responsibly' label on their bottles, I am making an 'improve responsibly' declaration on behalf of myself and my peers. I always remind my clients to put their strengths at the top of their mind and to focus on how they can develop and further enhance their positive qualities before looking at ways they can improve anything else.

When thinking about the things that you do want to improve, first make sure that your goals are reasonable and that you are not trying to be perfect or set yourself up to some exacting standard. Then ask yourself if improving this part of your life is really important to you … because if it doesn't really matter, why bother? And, finally, ask yourself what life would be like if you didn't change this part of your life at all.

While there might be things you would like to improve or change about yourself, remind yourself that it doesn't mean that there is anything wrong with the current version. Think of it like a software upgrade. The old version of Word works just fine; the newer version has just had a few tweaks and a couple of fancy new tricks added.

Once you are clear that you really do want to make positive changes in your life and make them for

the best possible reasons, you can begin your quest,
confident in the knowledge that you are enhancing
your true self, not eroding your self-esteem.

*Think of self-improvement like polishing
a diamond. You are already brilliant;
you just need to learn how to shine.*

Not every experience in a full, well-lived life is
going to be a beautiful one. Not every feeling is going
to be a loving one and not every aspect of a person
is going to be a lovely one. As a whole person, a
living breathing human being, not a two-dimensional
character created by an advertising agency or movie
company, you are multi-faceted. Some of those facets
will be brilliant and others less so.

The answer is to learn to love yourself for who
you are and all that you are, the good, the bad, the
weak, the strong, the ugly and the beautiful. Some
experiences in life are uplifting and others will make
you positively miserable. Anger is a healthy part of

life and a good cry usually comes with puffy eyes
and a runny nose (and for some reason in my case,
swollen lips). These are not the most beautiful parts
of ourselves or our experiences, but that doesn't
make them any less important.

Likewise, when it comes to an assessment of our
character or personal qualities, they won't all be
wonderful; we've all done things we're embarrassed
about, said things we shouldn't have and been less
than our best selves in one way or another. You
wouldn't be human if that wasn't the case. But rather
than beat yourself up, take some time to understand
what triggered your behaviour, how you can learn
from it or prevent it in the future, and whether or
not you need to make an apology. Once you've done
that, you can let it go. There is nothing to be gained
by agonising over your mistakes and kicking yourself
for things that you have gotten wrong or should have
done differently. Learn your lessons and move on.

If you find yourself making the same mistake over
and over, this still doesn't make you a bad person.
It just means you are not learning as quickly as you
might. Accepting your imperfections doesn't mean
you allow them to run rampant. If you find that some

of your character traits, habits or behaviours are less than desirable and that you really would benefit from conquering them, this is most definitely what you should aim to do. Just know that it doesn't mean you are a bad person who is trying to be good; you simply have attributes or qualities you would like to work on and improve.

If you strive for perfection you'll never be happy. If you focus on being happy, you won't care about being perfect.

Frank was a great salesman. In the competitive world of pharmaceutical sales his persistence, drive and determination stood him in good stead and he was consistently one of the top performers in his company. Frank knew that the answer to closing the deal was not to take no for an answer and instead to repackage or reposition his offer until it hit the mark with his client. He was comfortable with this approach and confident that it worked well for him … at least it did at work.

Most strengths have a flip side.
Learn to accept yours.

In his personal life, Frank was feeling unhappy and confused. He had separated from his wife the year before and, although he had dated a number of women, now that his divorce was finalised he was once again looking for a serious relationship.

He had been on a couple of first dates but each time he had proposed a second date Frank had been turned down. To someone who wasn't used to taking no for an answer, being on the receiving end of rejection was quite a shock and his confidence had taken a beating.

As I asked Frank to tell me a little bit more about these first dates it quickly became obvious where he was going wrong. Frank had approached these dates in much the same way he did a meeting at work. Although he had attempted to be charming and complimentary, what was successful in a sales meeting was coming across as overbearing, insistent and pushy over dinner for two.

When Frank first realised exactly how he had been going wrong he was embarrassed and told me he felt like a fool. Of course he wasn't a fool, but he did need to learn that what was a strength for him at work was not serving him well in his personal life, and that the flip side to being a great salesperson meant that he was often in 'sales mode' even when it wasn't appropriate.

Frank and I talked about how his other good qualities, like being quick to put someone at ease, being willing to laugh at himself and being thoughtful and considerate, would be more helpful qualities to call on when he was out on a date.

Frank went on a few more first dates. But this time he met a woman where the chemistry felt right, and his companion accepted his invitation to a second date, a third date and many more after that.

So often it is our very strengths that lead directly to our less-than-strong points. (I'm really not a fan of the term 'weakness' … unless we're talking about my weakness for chocolate fondant!) The outgoing person can become overwhelming, the strong leader is sometimes bossy, the highly organised person occasionally micro-manages, the nurturer becomes overly emotional and the person with an attention to detail finds themselves nitpicking over everything.

Instead of thinking of yourself as having strengths and weaknesses, think about your positive qualities, each of which has its own flip side. Once you realise that many of the things you are not so keen on about yourself are a direct or indirect result of the things you don't mind so much or even quite like, it becomes much easier to accept and even embrace your imperfections as an intrinsic part of what makes you you.

The **First Promise** is all about accepting yourself for who you are, in all your imperfect glory. Any time you find yourself striving for perfection, remind yourself that you are good enough exactly as you are. *Accept your imperfections* and commit to appreciating all of the qualities that make you you.

Always do your best

I always do my best and my best is always good enough.

When you consider your efforts, are you confident you have done your best?

Do you take a relaxed approach, picking and choosing when to expend your energy and when it is wiser to conserve it, knowing that as long as you do your best, your best will always be good enough? Or are you regularly in a state of exhaustion trying to do everything, be everything and have everything, worried that nothing you ever do will be good enough?

I've dedicated a whole book, *The Happiness Code*, to the importance of simply being the best you can be and how this is the key to lifelong happiness and fulfilment. Now I want to talk about why knowing that your best is good enough is so important for your confidence and self-esteem.

When nothing you do ever feels good enough, you exist in a constant state of dissatisfaction, frustration and disappointment … with yourself. Not a great foundation for building confidence! Deciding instead to be the best you can be is the most confidence-nurturing decision you can make. When you choose to be the best you can be, you are able to let go of any desire for perfection. You no longer need to prove yourself to others by 'winning' or being 'the best' at whatever it is you choose to do. Being the best you can be is about establishing your own benchmarks and making them your goal.

So many people misunderstand the difference between doing your best and feeling that there is nothing you can improve. But just because you aren't trying to be perfect doesn't mean you should become complacent about your efforts. Many people find the idea of giving up perfection as a goal a little daunting, but they are reassured when I tell them not to worry: they still need to do their best. The challenge now, however, is to work out what doing your best means to you.

It is rare that anyone ever finishes a task and can't see how it could be improved. For me, whether it's baking a cake or writing a book, as soon as I'm finished, I'm working out exactly what I would do differently to make it even better next time. 'What have you learned?' and 'What would you do differently next time?' are two of my favourite coaching questions. You can learn so much from your own experience, just by opening your eyes – but just because you can see how you would improve something doesn't mean that it isn't any good or that you haven't done your best. It just means that next time will be even better. Once you have stopped wasting your energy pursuing perfection, you are able to focus your effort on what it really means to do *your* best.

There is a big difference between doing your best and needing to be the best.

Every time you finish something that matters, ask yourself, 'What went well, what didn't go so well and what will I do differently next time?' Your answers to these questions will not only help you to improve, they will also see your confidence soar as your belief in the power of your own wisdom and insight grows.

Discovering room for improvement doesn't mean you didn't do your best. It just means that next time your best will be even better.

Life is not an Olympic sport; it's not a competition with only one winner and where a lifetime's worth of training all comes to a head in one event. For the most part, life offers the opportunity for continual improvement and it really doesn't matter what anyone else has achieved or how well they are doing. The only race you need to run is yours; what matters is how you feel about how *you* are doing.

Sometimes when you look around and see the progress other people are making, it can be hard not to feel intimidated or overwhelmed. Don't fall into the trap of thinking this makes the other person better than you. Leave everyone else to work out what their best looks like and remind yourself that all that matters is that you do *your best*.

Don't be intimidated by someone else's achievements. Do your best and don't worry about the rest.

Take the time to work out what your best effort looks like on a case-by-case basis. Not everything you do will require 110 per cent effort. Not everything needs to be brilliant or exceptional in some way. In some cases the best you will need to do is simply to get it done – just because you have the potential to do more doesn't mean you actually need to do more.

If you try to be brilliant at everything, no matter how big or small, important or insignificant, not only will you exhaust yourself physically, but with such an impossible goal, you will leave your self-confidence in tatters. Every time you consciously let yourself down, you chip away at your self-esteem.

*Don't set yourself up for failure
before you even begin.*

So many people subconsciously erode their self-confidence by setting themselves up for failure before they even begin. I don't just mean with big things – hopes, dreams and goals – I mean everyday objectives too … the to-do list that's never going to get done, the restrictive diet you're never going to stick to, the exercise regime that's impossible to fit in, the budget you won't follow and the commitments you know you can't keep.

Instead of trying to be the Invincible Woman (or Man), take the time to think about what it is that you really do need to achieve and what resources you have available to achieve it with. Most things need time, money, energy or a combination of all three. If you take the time to consider your available resources before you begin something, whether it's tackling your to-do list or something far more complicated, you will have a far greater chance of succeeding. Nothing builds your confidence quite as quickly as being able to say, 'I did it.'

If you try to do the impossible,
it will be impossible to succeed.

Considering the available resources has been something I've needed to focus on over the last few years. I have always been an ambitious person. I have big goals for my working life, but I am also ambitious for the rest of my life; the quality of my relationship, the way I parent, and my health and wellbeing sit at the top of my list. When I was 'young, free and single'

and otherwise unencumbered, if I had something I was focussing on at work, I could give it my all. One hundred per cent of my resources. There was nobody else I needed to consider, no compromises I needed to make and nobody I would be letting down if I didn't come home when I said I would or if I needed to work through the weekend.

But my life looks different now. I have a deeply committed relationship that deserves to be nurtured and two young children who want and need my attention. I still give my work my best, but that best is a very different shape than it was ten years ago when I started my business. And I'm okay with that, because I've taken the time to work out what the best I can be at work looks like. I've also had to consider what the best I can be looks like in every other part of life.

Although Andrea was a naturally happy person, when I first met her she was tired, angry and frustrated. A lifelong goal-setter, Andrea had always had a plan. She had a plan for her day, a plan for her week, for her year and of course a five-year plan to boot. But things weren't going to plan. Back at work a year after the maternity leave she had taken when her son was born, she had just found out she had been passed over for a promotion.

Andrea was quite emotional as she tried to explain just how upset missing out on this job made her feel. She said she had been all but killing herself trying to do a good job at work while juggling her responsibilities as a mother, and this setback was an insult to her efforts. At the same time, a part of her was relieved that she wouldn't have to do all the travelling this new job would have involved – but then she felt angry with herself for feeling that way, knowing what an important step this new job would have been in achieving her master plan. To put it plainly, her feelings were all over the place.

Be realistic about your resources
and do the best you can
with what you've got.

The first thing I asked Andrea to do was put her plans to the side for a moment and instead reconnect with her values. I reminded her that while she had career values, these needed to be compatible, rather than in conflict, with the values she held for her whole life. When Andrea got back to basics and thought about the things that mattered most to her in life, she realised she had been kidding herself to think that her five-year plan was still realistic. Her life had changed a lot since she had first written it and, while it was still technically achievable, it simply wasn't realistic for her if she was to honour her values for the rest of her life.

She felt relieved to know that she wasn't 'off her game'; it was simply that her game had changed. Andrea was still ambitious for her career but she now realised that those ambitions needed to fit in with the rest of her life. She still wanted to achieve most of the things on her original five-year plan, but was happy if her plan took somewhat longer to come to fruition.

It's easy to use the example of children as the source of parameters or boundaries. No-one ever questions the commitment of a parent who needs to leave work at a certain time because they have children to collect – of course you can't leave your children waiting. But if you don't have children, you still have every right to put boundaries and parameters in place that prevent your work from taking over the rest of your life. Regardless of your circumstances, take the time to consider the other commitments and priorities in your life and decide what your best needs to be in each individual situation.

Be realistic, not only about your available resources, but also about the effort level required. I always remind my clients that even at the best schools and universities, 80 per cent gets you an 'A'. You don't need to give a 150 per cent effort to prove to yourself (or anyone else for that matter) that you are trying to do a good job.

There is a big difference between a first-class effort and a foolish level of effort.

Sometimes, no matter how hard you try, your best might not be that great. It could be that you have underestimated your available resources; who hasn't left something to the last minute only to realise you would've done a much better job if you had started your project sooner? Perhaps, try as you might, you just weren't able to get your efforts to align with your intentions.

Sometimes your best will be a bit average and that is okay. When this happens, protect your self-esteem and forgive yourself for being less than brilliant. You are only human. Sometimes you will succeed, sometimes you will fail and sometimes you will stagger across the finish line just as they're packing up the race. Regardless of the outcome, as long as you have done your best, your best has been good enough.

There are no gold medals to be won in the game of life.

For many people, being released from the burden of striving for brilliance *all of the time* is an incredible relief. If this sounds like you and you've been exhausting yourself trying to be amazing at everything, always, you can stop, take a deep breath and relax. When you are ready to get started again, you can be confident in the knowledge that your best will be different for different things and on different occasions and, as long as you do your best, that will be all that matters.

How good is good enough is a conversation I regularly have with first-time mothers, women who are putting themselves under enormous pressure to be the perfect mum. The sleep deprivation combined with all of the other challenges of motherhood is enough to drive anyone crazy, but throw in the burden of perfectionism and there is really no way anyone can expect to survive unscathed.

When I became a mother for the first time, I took an altogether more relaxed approach. Please don't take this the wrong way. I take being a good mother very seriously, but I didn't (and still don't) let myself get defeated by the details. I believe a newborn has only five fundamental needs: to be fed, to be clothed and sheltered, to sleep, to be comforted and to be loved. And this is what I set out to do. I still read many of the same books on parenting as my girlfriends, but I didn't judge my success at mothering on my ability to implement the strategies and suggestions contained within. From my perspective all the popular titles were simply offering variations on how best to implement these five fundamentals. As long as I was doing my best to meet these needs, regardless of how I went about it, I was doing a good job.

Like any new mother, for me some days went well, some were disastrous and many went by in such a fog of fatigue that I don't remember what they were. But through it all, I remained kind to myself. I didn't expect perfection of myself, or for that matter my child. I was able to enjoy those crazy, early days far more than many women do, largely because I knew I was doing my best and that my best was good enough.

Actress and founder of The Honest Company, Jessica Alba, agrees. 'I wish there were two of me and 48-hour days so I could get everything done,' she told *Parade*. 'But for me, I have to not try and think that everything has to be 100 per cent perfect all the time and leave room for error. As long as my kids feel loved and a priority, everything else really is secondary.' Wise words from a very busy woman.

When things don't go your way, whether it is as simple as forgetting to do something you said you were going to do or more significant like missing out on a promotion at work, don't view it as a failure. Instead, be kind to yourself and recognise the effort that you made, regardless of the end result. Don't think of yourself as a failure. There are often many things at play that are beyond your control, but the thing you can control is your effort, and as long as you've given the situation the effort it deserves, then you have every reason to be happy with yourself.

You are good enough.
FACT.

Remind yourself that everyone fails sometime. Actually, it is a recognised fact that the more successful someone is, the more often they will have failed along the way. Failing, or simply not getting something right, doesn't make you less of a person. It doesn't make *you* a failure. It just means that whatever you were doing, whether it's baking a cake or starting a business, simply hasn't succeeded yet.

You are not a share on the stock market; your value is not determined by your performance.

When things don't go your way, it's never a pleasant experience. I don't care how many times Richard Branson or any other successful entrepreneur has failed, I bet he (or she) has never *enjoyed* the experience. Knowing that even your best efforts didn't quite make the grade can be painful. Depending on what was at stake it might be annoying, embarrassing, frustrating, humiliating, stressful, overwhelming or heartbreaking and, whatever feelings you experience, it's important that you do experience them and don't hide from them or deny them.

Many people mistakenly believe that in order to be a positive and happy person, you should ignore or brush over your disappointments and setbacks, but I don't agree. Or at least I don't fully agree. While I think it's important not to dwell on your setbacks or languish in your disappointment, it is important to both acknowledge and experience your feelings. All of your feelings. Left ignored, negative feelings can fester and become debilitating, or turn into overwhelming fears if we try to hide from them.

Don't hang out in the dark zone of disappointment any longer than you need to. Help your confidence recover from the knock it has taken by acknowledging your feelings, learning what you can from the situation and then moving on and getting back to your authentic happy state as quickly as possible.

You know that old saying, 'If at first you don't succeed, try, try again' … well, I want to add something to it: 'if you want to'. So often people attempt something, don't succeed and then place themselves under incredible pressure to push and push themselves in the hope that they might eventually succeed. While it's important to have the will and tenacity to pursue the things that really matter in your life, you don't need to apply this approach to every single thing you attempt.

Michael had begun his career as a lawyer but he had always harboured a secret dream of owning and managing a wine bar, and the year he turned forty he decided to take the plunge. He resigned his partnership from a prestigious law firm and set about opening the coolest wine bar in town.

When I met Michael he was at a crossroads. His wine bar had been open for a year and while he had enjoyed many of the benefits of being in the industry (regular wine tastings, for one!) he really wasn't enjoying himself at all. Although he had experience working on huge deals where millions of dollars were at stake, he found the financial management of a small business stressful. Even though it had received good reviews the wine bar was barely breaking even, and Michael was having to 'watch the pennies' in a way he never had to when he worked at the big end of town.

He found it hard to get the right staff and, although he came from a legal background where he was no stranger to hard work, he felt like he was working all day and night for very little reward. While he enjoyed the company of some of his regular customers, he found others to be rude and dismissive, not to mention drunk.

When I asked Michael if he had thought about closing the wine bar and going back to the law firm, he was shocked. It really hadn't occurred to him – as he explained, he was 'no quitter'. Michael and I spent some time exploring the difference between quitting and giving up and deciding that something wasn't working and moving on.

As painful as it is, it really doesn't matter if you fall down. All that matters is how quickly you can dust yourself off and get back up again.

It might seem strange at first, but there really is nothing wrong with trying something, finding that you crash and burn, dusting yourself and your ego off and walking away. You don't need to stick around and conquer every single thing in life. Life is not a battle to be won, it's a journey to be experienced. And sometimes what you gain in the attempt is the insight to know that you don't actually want or need what you once were chasing.

Although initially worried about being seen as a 'failure' in his friends' and former colleagues' eyes, Michael soon realised that closing the wine bar and going back to being a lover of wine, not a server of wine, was the right step forward for him.

Life is not a battle to be won.
It is a journey to be experienced.

Everyone has good days, when everything comes together with the greatest of ease, and not-so-great days, when everything feels like an uphill battle from the moment you get out of bed in the morning to the time you get back in at night. Having a bad day is a normal part of life and just because things aren't going right, it doesn't mean there is anything wrong with you. Don't allow the way you feel about a task, situation or circumstance define how you feel about yourself.

One of the most common questions I am asked is, 'Does being a writer about happiness mean you

never feel unhappy? Do you ever have a bad day?'
Of course I do – I'm human too! But I do make sure
that I don't let a bad day turn into a bad week, a bad
week into a bad month, or bad month into a bad year.
I don't allow having a negative experience to make me
feel negatively about myself.

When you truly believe your best is good enough,
you can accept that you are having a bad day, or
feeling a bit ordinary, without this affecting the way
you feel about your*self*.

The **Second Promise** is all about simply doing
your best. Whenever you find you are holding on to
unrealistic expectations and setting yourself up for
failure, remind yourself that your self-worth is based
on who you are, not what you can or can't do. Make
the commitment to *always do your best and know that
your best is always good enough.*

Stop comparing yourself

I have no need to see myself as more or less than anyone else.

When you look in the mirror, what do you see?

Do you see someone who is intelligent, thoughtful, and worthy of love and happiness? Or do you see someone who isn't as attractive, slim, rich, successful, well-dressed, fit or clever as other people you know?

While in reality you are likely to be a mix of both, most people don't focus on the first component, their positive attributes, because they're too busy listing all the deficiencies instead. But your faults don't lie in the things you perceive as missing when you compare yourself to others … the fault is engaging in the act of comparison in the first place.

This unhelpful habit of comparing yourself to others was probably initiated way back in your school years. Back then you were constantly being graded by your teacher, making it very clear to you exactly where you sat on the scale. Such rigorous comparison is potentially helpful in an educational environment, where bell curves, standard deviations and other statistical measures are used to prove teaching methods are having their desired effect. However, as an adult you are responsible for your own life lessons, the gaining of wisdom, your emotional wellbeing and your physical health. Comparing yourself to others serves no benefit and does nothing except erode your self-esteem and undermine your confidence.

Some people will have more and have done more than you. Others will be slimmer and fitter. Many will have more of the things you desire. But the only healthy response to this is, 'So what?'

Just as you may look at someone and see things they have that make you feel *less than* or inadequate in some way, the same people are no doubt looking at others (and potentially even you) and seeing all of the things they believe are missing from their own lives. Nobody's life is perfect, no-one has everything and unless you are Bill Gates, Warren Buffet or Oprah, someone is bound to have more money than you.

There is no upside to comparing yourself to others, only the downside of watching your confidence disappear.

As we each follow our individual paths in life, we are faced with opportunities and choices. Each person will have different priorities, make different choices and end up with different outcomes based on their life values, past experiences and future goals. Comparing yourself to others usually involves focussing on their upside and your downside. This is hardly a balanced perspective. Not only is this kind of comparison destructive to your self-esteem, it's also an inaccurate perception of reality.

Consider marriage. One person may marry for love, but feel they never have enough spare money for the holidays they would like to take. Another person may choose a partner for security, but feel that there is a lack of passion in their life. Everyone knows a story of a seemingly perfect couple who shock their friends and family with the announcement of their separation. Naively everyone is astonished to find that things were not as they had seemed. Marriage is just one of myriad examples. I could have just as easily said career, home, children, fitness, physique or lifestyle. When you compare yourself to others, you end up focussing on what they have and what you don't, without acknowledging the whole picture. And there's always more to the picture.

In life there is always the good stuff
and then there is the rest of it.

Never is this more apparent than in celebrity gossip. Who is wearing what, who has gained weight, lost weight, coupled up, broken up, is pregnant, might be pregnant, lost the baby weight, got drunk, got sober, had a hit, had a flop.

Remember, there is always
more to the picture.

Every time you read about celebrities we are only ever reading what they or the publication in question want you to read. *Actress works out diligently, eats low-calorie, healthy diet and eventually loses weight* won't sell magazines. Nor does *Singer starves herself, gets constipated, has bad breath but loses weight quickly before putting it back on just as fast.* These are not popular stories. So what gets presented to us is, *Movie star looks amazing, having lost weight with incredible ease, eating what she wants and engaging in a light exercise routine, mostly consisting of pole dancing.* Readers lap this content up, saying to themselves, 'Wow, so that's how she did it …' which is invariably followed by,

'What's wrong with me, why can't I do that, why doesn't it work that way for me?'

Everything we read has been spun, posed and Photoshopped. Publicists pitch stories designed to sell movie tickets and records, to get people to buy products and ultimately to ensure their clients are perceived in a certain light. Meanwhile magazines, newspapers and even bloggers have brainstorming sessions to come up with cover stories they think will sell. The cover stories are decided first; the facts are collated second. The end result for the reader is largely fiction and the result of significant creative endeavour. No-one understood this better than Elvis Presley, who said, 'The image is one thing and the human being is another. It's very hard to live up to an image, put it that way.'

Occasionally 'brave' celebrities share the 'truth': Jennifer Lopez tells us how hard she worked out to maintain her figure, Kate Winslet poses for *Vanity Fair* without make-up and Jessica Simpson explains exactly how she got her post-baby body back. But for the most part, what is shared is only a part of the reality and this 'honesty' has been communicated with the primary aim of having the celebrity perceived in a certain light: as the dedicated performer, the authentic actress and the girl next door.

Celebrity gossip has been created for our entertainment. We shouldn't believe it any more than we believe Wonder Woman really flew an invisible plane or Superman came from a planet called Krypton. Enjoy it with a light-hearted humour or avoid it altogether, but whatever you do, don't compare yourself to it.

Comparing yourself to a celebrity is no different to comparing yourself to any other fictional character.

While comparing yourself to glamorous celebrities who are presented as perfect is unhealthy, it is equally toxic to consume stories about Z-list celebrities and their train-wreck lives. The stories of drunken behaviour, promiscuity, addiction and obesity can make compelling reading but comparing yourself to this, in this way, is almost as toxic as the behaviour you are reading about.

Comparing yourself to others, coming off second best and feeling inadequate have an immediate negative impact on your confidence and self-esteem. Finding entertainment in other people's misfortune isn't healthy either. While you might experience the short-term high that comes from thinking, 'Well it's not all bad – at least my life doesn't look like theirs', this is only giving your self-esteem a false boost until the next thing that makes you feel inadequate comes along.

Comparing yourself to someone else won't make you feel good about yourself.

Comparing yourself against the profile and newsfeeds of people you know, sort of know or used to know, can be just as harmful to your confidence as comparing yourself to people in the public eye.

Modern social media platforms give everyday people the chance to manage their 'public perception' in much the same way as a celebrity does. You can choose what stories you want to tell, select your images, crop them, put a filter on them and then share them with the world.

I love sharing on Facebook and Instagram pictures of delicious things I have baked, but I'll be honest, it has never occurred to me to post pictures of the things that I've been disappointed in or that have flopped. Am I a good cook? Sure. But if you check out the photos I share, you could be forgiven for thinking I'd like to give Martha Stewart or Donna Hay a run for their money. And while I'm giving my secrets away, the reason I only post pictures of wonderful food and beautifully laid tables every now and then is because I only cook an extravagant meal or bake an amazing cake every now and then. The rest of the time the menu at our house is pretty simple, but if you based your perception on my Instagram feed, you could be forgiven for thinking that this is what all mealtimes look like Chez Moi.

Likewise when you read about acquaintances, old schoolfriends and exes on social media, they are

only telling or showing you what they want you to
see and hear.

Don't believe everything you read,
see or hear. It's usually only a
small slice of the truth.

There is nothing wrong with wanting to present
yourself to the world in the best possible light. Nor
is there anything wrong with only wanting to share
the good parts of your life with virtual strangers,
and saving the 'whole' story for just your closest
friends and family. The problem lies with the reader's
perception. As a reader, it is your responsibility to
remember that what you are reading is usually only
a small part of the reality. If you compare yourself
to what you see on social media not only will you
be doing your confidence a grave disservice, your
assessment will have been based on a somewhat
distorted version of reality.

Of course there are just as many real-life train wrecks on social media as there are in celebrity life and, in the same way, focussing on what you think people are getting wrong or failing at is not good for your self-esteem: the high school heartthrob who now looks like an oaf, the queen of the 'in crowd' who has obviously lost her crown or the ex who makes you think, 'Look who's sorry now.' The thrill you get from these updates might give your ego a quick boost but it's a hollow, worthless thrill.

Thinking you are better than someone else will only make you feel good until it starts to feel bad.

I remember seeing, when Facebook began gaining popularity, a picture of a girl I went to school with, who had always been super slim and sporty, looking somewhat large and wobbly. I'm human, I'm fallible, and the honest truth is I got a cheap thrill from seeing how much she had changed. I still remember the icky, almost ashamed feeling I had when I discovered that the flab I had taken delight in seeing was the result of her having given birth just a few weeks before. Of course her tummy wobbled; this woman had just brought life into the world. My thrill was short lived and did nothing but leave me feeling bad about myself.

Actress and author of *The Body Book*, Cameron Diaz, knows how important it is not to compare yourself to other people. As she told *Vogue*:

> We are all different, and we all wish we had something other than what we have. What we women need to do, instead of worrying about what we don't have, is just love what we do have. Get to know your body. Love it, respect it, treat it right. And in return you'll be happier with you.

Whether it's celebrities, our closest friends or people we used to know, comparing yourself to others is never healthy. If you are lucky, you get the short-lived, false high that comes from feeling superior … but most of the time your comparison will leave you feeling inferior, insignificant or inadequate.

In the countries in which I've spent the most time living, Australia and the United Kingdom, anything that can be seen as boasting or big-noting yourself is frowned upon. At the same time self-deprecation is all but encouraged. But while humility (never seeing yourself as better or more important than anyone else) is a desirable quality, having an inferiority complex where you see everyone as being better than you won't do you any favours either.

Enjoying the misfortune of others
is toxic to your self-esteem.

Monica was a client of mine who ran a catering company. What had started out as a small business that she ran from her own kitchen had morphed into a much larger company with a commercial kitchen and ten full-time staff. The business was well and truly profitable, the staff were loyal and the clients were happy.

Monica still wasn't sure she was getting it right. Although she had trained as a chef, she had never studied business and a part of her couldn't believe that *she* had created this success. She kept talking about how much more other people in her industry knew and how 'lucky' she was. Although I regularly reminded her of one of my favourite quotes, 'The harder you work the luckier you get', she still wasn't convinced.

When a new corporate contract meant that Monica needed to employ another staff member she was quick to hire a 'young gun' she had interviewed, who had previously worked for a much larger company than hers. She thought this would be a great opportunity for her to gain some insight into how bigger companies got things done, and she shared this at the interview.

Monica's natural management style was gentle and nurturing and until now it had served her well with the staff who had grown with her as her business had grown. Unfortunately things weren't going well with the new recruit, who had taken the idea that she was to share her insights and interpreted it as permission to tell everyone what to do and try to fix things that weren't broken. Each time Monica tried to discuss this, the new recruit shot her back down with industry statistics and jargon.

As she began to feel her already shaky confidence wither, Monica realised she would need to change her approach. The humility that had once appeared to serve her well had now become a detriment and she reluctantly realised she would need to step more fully into her role as the leader of her business. Together we built a list of all Monica had learned and how much she had achieved since starting her business. Seeing her wisdom and success on paper allowed Monica to feel proud of her achievements and gave her the confidence to lead her business in the way she knew was best.

Of course nobody wants to be around an egomaniac – someone who is constantly big-noting themselves or blowing their own trumpet – but humility can be a false friend if you take it too far. There is a fine line between not believing in your own importance and not believing you are important, in not being proud versus being proud of what you've done, between seeing the value in everyone and failing to see the value in yourself.

Understand the difference between humility and inferiority. One will nurture your self-esteem and the other will destroy it.

While I am a big believer in not taking yourself too seriously, constantly mocking yourself or putting yourself down with a never-ending stream of self-deprecating comments belongs in a comedy routine – where it is designed to be followed by a big, loud, confidence-affirming round of applause – not in your day-to-day life.

Being able to laugh warmheartedly when faced with your failings is a wonderful confidence-enhancing quality, but there is a fine line between not taking yourself too seriously and making yourself the butt of the joke. Constantly mocking yourself or putting yourself down achieves nothing except the slow and steady erosion of your self-esteem.

Everyone is on a different journey in life. Depending on your path, there might be any number of things you still want to have or achieve and you may find yourself comparing your progress against others.

Your life might not be perfect and you may see examples of people around you who are doing, being or having more of what you want. If you find yourself tempted to engage in comparison, instead of allowing your assessment to diminish or deflate your self-esteem, switch your perspective.

Being able to laugh at yourself enhances your confidence. Mocking yourself erodes it.

If you find you are comparing yourself with someone who has something you want, instead of letting yourself feel bad, inadequate or *less than* in some way, use their experience as proof that what you want is possible. Don't allow yourself to give in to jealousy or become intimidated. Instead, reframing your comparison allows this person to become your inspiration.

A short while back I found myself momentarily comparing myself to a colleague whose blog had really taken off. This woman had recently suffered a devastating loss and it was her raw honesty as she waded through her grief that had brought readers flocking to her site. For a fleeting moment I found myself feeling envious of her success. I say fleeting, because the realisation that I was coveting the success of someone who had recently lost her husband made any symptoms of my envy evaporate immediately.

The fact that someone else has what you want is not cause for complaint. It is proof that it is possible and cause for celebration.

Remind yourself that this other person doesn't have something you want because they are better than you, more worthy than you or luckier than you. They have it because it's their time to have it, because having it now fits with the life journey they are on.

In nearly every case imaginable, you too will be able to get most of what you want in life. It won't always happen when you want it and it might not happen exactly the way you hope, but if you do your part and put in the groundwork, effort and commitment, more often than not, you will eventually get what you want.

Passing judgement is really just another form of negative comparison. If you find yourself comparing yourself with someone who is less fortunate than you or going through a difficult time in their life, whether that's someone you know, a social media 'friend' or a celebrity you follow, instead of using their misfortune or difficulties to artificially inflate your ego, use your awareness as an opportunity to express your gratitude for the positivity, abundance and wellbeing in your life.

Whenever I read about poverty or suffering, I say to myself, 'I am so lucky that my biggest problem is… [insert First World problem here].' If I find myself drawn to a celebrity's misfortune or suffering, I remind myself that I am so fortunate to be able to make my mistakes and experience my suffering in the relative privacy and anonymity of my life. And, if someone I know or used to know is doing it tough,

I reach for that age-old expression, 'there but for the grace of God, go I'. Which really just means 'it's the luck of the draw that it was them not me, so count your blessings'.

Instead of comparing yourself and finding yourself wanting, count your blessings and remember all that you have to be grateful for.

All too often, I see people measure their self-worth by their net worth or some other erroneous scale. You are not the value of your assets any more than you are the value of your achievements.

Victor was used to making money. He had started his career selling bags of sweets to his friends at the age of twelve and had never looked back. Victor had a beautiful home, a lovely wife and two gorgeous children. But he was tired. Closer to fifty than forty, he wanted to be able to take his foot off the accelerator and enjoy the simple things in life, like being able to walk his daughters to school, meet his wife for lunch or take off for a fishing trip, instead of always jetting off to close his next big deal.

Victor still wanted to enjoy the good things in life – he wasn't about to sell everything and live in a yurt – but he was ready to start planning the next stage in his life, and he asked me to help him explore his options.

Although he didn't put it in so many words, Victor's biggest concern was how much of his identity was tied up with his professional success. He said things like, 'But if I'm not the CEO of my company, who am I?' and 'Will people still look at me the same way if I'm not the guy at the top?' Victor and I talked about how much of his self-worth had been tied to his business success and how he would need to find a new source of confidence if he was to feel good about himself once he had said goodbye to his company.

Slowly Victor came to realise that his successes didn't define him any more than the occasional failure had; that just as earning more than most of his friends hadn't made him better than them, earning less wouldn't make him less than them either. He learned not to source his confidence from the job he chose to do, and instead from the person he chose to be.

When you compare yourself to others you invariably wind up feeling like you don't measure up. You are intelligent, thoughtful and deserving of love and happiness, and nothing that anyone else has or does changes this fact. Instead of comparing yourself to others and feeling like you fall short, decide to be the measure of your own greatness and boost your confidence by reflecting on all the happiness, successes and rewarding moments, big or small, you have had in your life so far.

Set simple goals for yourself that you know you can confidently achieve. Achieve them and then enjoy measuring your own progress from who you were to who you are becoming. What matters is who you are, not what you have or the things you've done. Life is not a competition. No-one can win and no-one will lose … but some people will enjoy it a whole lot more, simply because they feel better about themselves. Source your confidence from within and base it not on what you think about everyone else, but what you know to be true about yourself.

The **Third Promise** is all about valuing yourself for who you are and not how you compare to someone else. Whenever you find yourself thinking you are better or worse than someone, remind yourself all that matters is how good you feel about yourself. Make the commitment to *stop comparing yourself to others* and source your confidence from within.

Believe in your potential

I fully expect my life to be happy and rewarding.

When you think of your future, how do you see it turning out?

Do you see your future as being full of possibilities? Do you see a life where the majority of the things you want have come or are coming your way? Where your heart is full of love and there is an abundance of happiness?

Or do you find that, while you might hope all of this *will* be true, far too much of your energy is spent worrying that it won't be? Worrying about things that have happened, things that might happen and even things that will probably never happen?

Worrying is a destructive habit. It can be both consuming and exhausting, but for all the energy it absorbs it offers you nothing in return. Not only is worrying a waste of energy, it also sends a clear message to your subconscious about your expectations in life. When you worry things might go wrong, your subconscious interprets this as an expectation that things *will* go wrong.

If you can do something about it, do it.
If you can't, let it go.

There are only two kinds of situations in life: those you have influence over or can do something about, and those that you can't. If you can do something about a situation, make a change, prevent an outcome or remedy an event, then you should. But if you can't significantly influence or change the outcome, then regardless of how unpleasant or awful the risks might be, you need to find a way to accept them. You don't have to like it, but you still have to accept it.

Unless you have a crystal ball, you don't know how the future will unfold. Continuing to worry about an event or outcome over which you have no control will leave you feeling churned up and turned inside out and yet has absolutely no positive impact at all. Why not assume things are going to turn out for the best and save your energy for improving or rectifying things on the odd occasion that they don't?

No amount of worry is going to determine the outcome, regardless of the situation you find yourself in. Instead of thinking around and around in circles about how things might turn out, put your energy to much better use by planning and preparing for the best possible outcome. This could be anything from preparing as well as you can for an important meeting, booking a preventative health screening or teaching your children about personal safety.

You can't make someone give you the job or force your boss to like your report, but what you can do is plan, prepare and put your energy toward doing the best job you possibly can. There is no point worrying you might get cancer or some other deadly sickness. Book your health screenings in annually (I do mine around my birthday so I never forget) and make sure that any health blips that come your way are picked up and dealt with as soon as possible. Make good diet, exercise and lifestyle choices and take care of your body the best you possibly can in between these appointments.

Being prepared is the best investment you can make in your future.

Mia was always worrying about something. She worried if she was doing a good enough job at work, at home and just about everywhere in between. When she heard that a neighbour's children were ill, she worried her children would catch it. When she heard about a friend being made redundant she worried she would be next. In fact Mia was so busy worrying about her life that she barely had time to enjoy it.

I met Mia when she attended one of my workshops. Throughout the course of the day she told me she had worried that everyone else would be cleverer and more together than she was, that I would be scary and intimidating in real life and that she would be the fattest person in the room. Of course none of these things were true; Mia fitted in perfectly and had a fabulous time.

One of the exercises in the workshop was to identify the different ways you hold yourself back from achieving your potential. Mia had the insight to see that worrying about what could go wrong was definitely getting in her way but she didn't know where to begin in breaking this unhelpful habit.

I asked Mia to undertake a little experiment. I wanted her to pretend nothing in her life could go wrong for a whole week. She didn't need to do anything other than exchange her worried thoughts for new positive ones; she didn't need to believe it, but every time she found herself worrying, she simply needed to do it.

When I checked in with Mia it was like talking to a new person. She was so much more relaxed and happy. I asked her what had changed and she said when she stopped worrying and nothing had actually changed, it made her realise how little impact her worries had been having and how much energy she had been wasting. She had finally realised that her worries had been a bad habit and not based on any truth.

Worry is not a sign of love.
It is a symptom of fear.

Although she hadn't fully broken the habit, now when Mia found herself worrying she was able to snap out of it quickly and go back to assuming that everything would turn out all right in her world.

I once read a quote that said having a child was like having your heart live outside of yourself. Having children definitely opens you up to myriad new opportunities for concern, but worrying is not a sign of love; it is a symptom of fear. No matter how much you love your children it is up to you how much you are going to worry about them.

Instead of worrying yourself sick that something bad might happen to your children, and then diminishing their confidence by sharing your fears, do what you can to teach them how to be healthy, to be safe and how to protect themselves. Of course this approach doesn't offer any guarantees, but it provides you with a much better chance of a positive outcome than allowing yourself to be consumed with fear.

A couple of weeks after my 20th birthday, I quit university, packed up my things and moved from Perth to Sydney to pursue my modelling career. When I had been there about a fortnight, I met an unemployed actor who I fell madly in love with and proceeded to move in with a couple of weeks later. My poor parents! Of course at the time I didn't give their feelings a moment's thought. I was far too busy living *my life* and it wasn't until many years later when I had a child of my own that it occurred to me that it must have been a really challenging time for them.

Not so long ago, I asked my mother if she had been worried sick about me during that time. She wisely said that although she hadn't been particularly happy about my choices she had hoped that she had done a good job raising me, providing me with solid values, and that I had a clear enough head on my shoulders to ensure that my life would still turn out well, which of course it did.

Although my mother had her concerns, she was right not to worry. My parents had given me a really solid foundation and, while university-drop-out-shacked-up-with-unemployed-actor wasn't what they had envisioned for my 21st year, I did in fact continue to make relatively sensible choices, respect my values and keep myself out of any serious harm.

Although I never appreciated it at the time, their quiet acceptance of my choices provided great reinforcement – not only their unconditional love, but also the fact that while *they* might not like my decisions, they had confidence in my ability to make the right decisions for *me*.

As my confidence in my own decisions grew, it became obvious to me that I needed to end the relationship and move on with my life. In the end, despite how my initial foray into independence began, everything turned out okay. It might not have been ideal in parts, but the overall outcome was still a good one. While I would never suggest that my parents didn't feel concern for me at times, had they indulged in incessant worry and shared those worries with me it would have undermined my confidence and may have even made matters worse by giving me the feeling that I needed to rebel or prove them wrong in some other way.

Not everything in life will turn out perfectly. Sometimes things will go wrong and sometimes it will be your fault. Whether you've said the wrong thing in a social situation, let a friend or lover down, or made a mistake at work, don't fall into the trap of beating yourself up. Don't spend hours thinking about what you got wrong and why that makes you a bad person. It doesn't. You are the same *you*, you have just messed up in some way.

Don't worry about what everyone else thinks. Have confidence in your ability to make the right decision for you.

Instead of churning over things that have already happened, leading your mind around and around in circles as you agonise about how things might have been, challenge yourself to think in a more linear way. Ask yourself what went well, what didn't go so well and what you will do differently next time. Thinking in this linear way tells your subconscious that, although the outcome might not have turned out the way you wanted it to, you have the ability to learn – and this knowledge will give you the insight to do things differently next time.

One of the most powerful questions you can ask yourself is 'What will I do differently next time?'

Knowledge is power and thinking in this way, regardless of how disappointed or frustrated you might feel with yourself at the time, will ultimately have a powerful, confidence-boosting effect. Once you have found your insights, learned your lessons and considered what you will do differently next time, it is time to let it go. Forgive yourself. Don't agonise any further over what might have been. Put your chastising thoughts aside and direct your energy towards avoiding making the same mistake again.

Reminding yourself that you have the ability to grow, learn and continue to become an even better version of yourself is far more nurturing to your confidence and self-esteem than blasting yourself for your mistakes and engaging in endless rounds of self-criticism and abuse.

Everyone makes mistakes.
Learn from yours and then move on.

When you truly believe in your potential, making decisions in life becomes a whole lot easier. Instead of worrying about what might go wrong and letting your fears hold you back, you are able to consider the risks or worst-case scenario and calmly decide if you are prepared to move forward.

Feeling confident about your options doesn't mean you have to feel invincible. Believing that nothing ever can or will go wrong is surely a sign of delusion. Consider the worst-case scenario, but don't forget to give the best-case scenario just as much thought.

Some people mistakenly think being a positive person means you can only ever look on the bright side of life and that even contemplating negative outcomes will have a toxic and negative effect. I think the opposite is true. Blindly expecting life to turn out perfectly leaves you feeling incredibly vulnerable and exposed when things don't.

A far more sensible approach is to take the time to explore the worst-case scenario and to understand, firstly, how likely or unlikely it is, and then, secondly, whether or not you would be able to cope if it did happen. If your honest answer is that the worst-case scenario is too much to bear, then you have your answer: this option or opportunity that you are considering is not for you. You can retreat in confidence knowing that, for you, the risks were too high and that you are uncomfortable exposing yourself to something with that much potential for regret.

If, having considered the worst-case scenario, you feel that this outcome is not highly probable and is in fact something you would survive, or perhaps that living with the regret of not having attempted it would be worse, you can confidently make your decision to progress.

My good friend Kirsty Spraggon, creator and host of the online talk show Kirstytv.com, explained her decision to leave a highly successful career in Australia and move to Los Angeles to start her TV show like this:

> I knew I could live with the worst-case scenario – losing everything and having to go home and live with my parents – but I could never have lived with not giving it a go.

Knowing what you want to happen while being aware of what might happen leaves you feeling confident you can handle whatever *will* happen.

James wasn't a 'glass half empty' kind of guy, but he didn't exactly see the world through an optimistic lens either. Although he referred to himself as a realist, I thought his exterior happiness was simply disguising the negative perspective he carried inside.

James came to see me because he wanted to make some significant changes in his career. After living in New York for many years, he wanted to return home, but unfortunately the company he was working for didn't have an office in Australia. James was concerned about how hard it might be to find another job.

An intelligent man with a solid CV, James had a lot of things going for him but somehow he just couldn't wrench his mind away from his assessment of the worst-case scenario. In his mind, the worst thing that could happen was not only that he would remain unemployed indefinitely but that this could rapidly lead to losing all his savings and investments and leave him both penniless and homeless.

James and I discussed the option of not making any changes in his life if the risks felt too great, but deep down he knew that, despite his fears, doing nothing wasn't the right answer for him either. What he really needed to do was to find a way of breaking down the risks so he could assess them with a clearer, less emotive head.

I asked James to make a list of the decision-making points en route to the worst case becoming a reality:

he could do some research from his current home before he moved; he could set a time limit to make things work in Australia before deciding it wasn't working and heading back to New York where he knew there were plenty of jobs for people with his skills; and he could get a job in a bar or cafe to supplement his income if his financial reserves started to get too low. As he began to break his worst case down into stages, James was able to see he had a lot more control over the situation than he initially realised.

When you understand and accept the risks or downside associated with any situation, you free yourself up to focus on the outcome you do want to create. You can focus your *attention on your intention* and give your very best efforts mentally, emotionally and physically toward creating the outcome you both desire and deserve.

Once James realised that it was extremely unlikely he would arrive at his worst-case scenario without warning, and that he would have plenty of opportunity to avert the financial disaster he feared, he felt much more confident and was able to focus on the positive outcome he desired.

Numerous studies have shown that people who write down their goals have an exponentially greater chance of achieving them. Whether you believe in quantum physics, attraction theory, the power of goal setting or simply that being prepared allows you to make the most of your luck, it works. Focussing on what you want helps you to get it. At the same time if all your attention is on what can go wrong or why you might not get what you want, you increase the likelihood of a negative outcome.

Understand the risks,
but focus on your reward.

Your expectation or outlook affects the choices you make and the decisions you take, which in turn have a fundamental impact on the outcome. When you believe things are going to go your way, it is natural to work toward them, doing whatever it is that you need to do to bring the outcome you want closer to you.

As you achieve your goals your confidence grows, and as your confidence grows it becomes easier to believe in the things you are working towards. Believing in your potential becomes a self-fulfilling prophecy of the best possible kind.

When you focus on what you want
you exponentially increase
your chance of getting it.

Your perspective is the single biggest influence on your experiences. How you expect something to be actually has an impact on how it will be. Now I'm not saying you have the power to win the lottery or to control the weather. Just because you expect your numbers to come up doesn't mean they will; just because you expect it to rain on Saturday it doesn't mean you shouldn't wash your car. But have you noticed that if you believe you are going to have a good time you usually will? And, likewise, that if you think the worst of someone you will usually be able to find something about them to back up your theory?

My favourite example of the power of your perspective is the weather. You can't control the weather; all you can control is your experience of it. When the weather gets in the way of your plans there really are only two ways you can look at it: you can see your day as being ruined and add to the downpour with your tears as you watch your plans wash away, or you can seize the moment and look at the inclement weather as a chance to watch a movie you've been meaning to see, cuddle up on the sofa with a good book, or head to a pub for a cosy all-afternoon lunch.

You choose your experience.

Whenever something goes wrong in your life, you can always look for the silver lining. Many people are fond of the expression 'everything happens for a reason'. I'm not 100 per cent sure that's what I believe … I think sometimes things just happen.

But regardless of which is true, what I do know for certain is that it is your responsibility to find the reason, meaning or lesson in any given event.

Even the happiest, richest and most rewarding life will have heartache, disappointment and sadness. Not every experience in your life will be a good one, but when you believe that you deserve a happy and fulfilling life, you will be able to move through these darker times quicker and with greater ease than if you believe the opposite to be true.

Expect your life to be happy
and it will be.

You don't need to be relentlessly positive to put this into action in your life. Believing that you deserve to live a happy and rewarding life doesn't exclude you from life's ups and downs. You're still allowed to have a bad day. And you are still allowed to fully explore all the thoughts and feelings, including

the less-than-positive ones, you might have about
an experience.

When you force yourself to feel positive all the
time, it's like staying up all night on caffeine – you are
doing nothing but setting yourself up for an almighty
crash. It's perfectly normal to have fear, doubt or
uncertainty. There is nothing wrong with experiencing
negative thoughts or feelings – what matters is the
power you give them.

Allow your negative thoughts or feelings to present
themselves, acknowledge them and recognise any
value they bring or investigation they warrant, and
then let them go. It's important that you see fear as a
healthy part of life, but also recognise that it doesn't
have to have power over your life. Experience your
fears and other 'negative' emotions but don't submit
to them or allow them to consume you or otherwise
influence your decisions.

The same goes for the experiences you've had that
haven't gone your way. I'd love to promise you that
once you believe in yourself everything will go your
way from this point onwards … and hey, maybe for
you it will. But my experience is that even though
believing in yourself means that *more* things go your

way, life is still going to throw you a curve ball from time to time. It is important that you see this for what it is and don't view your disappointments or let-downs as a sign of things to come, leading you into a spiral of negativity that only serves to undermine your self-belief.

*Don't allow your negative feelings
to hold the power in your life.*

Any full and interesting life is bound to have a range of ups and downs, but sometimes people allow a past experience to define their future expectations: the broken heart that leads you to believe that you are unlucky in love, the promotion that goes to someone else and leaves you thinking 'I'll never make the grade' or that 'good things only happen to other people'. Leave your past in the past and decide what you want your future to be like. Once you've made that decision, put your effort and your intentions into making it your reality.

Decide what you want your future to be like, then put your effort and your intentions into making it your reality.

Learn to believe in your potential. Why shouldn't you be living your best possible life? Recall the expression 'fake it till you make it' and treat your self-belief the same way. Tell yourself, often enough and for long enough, that you believe in your potential – and sooner or later you will.

Whatever it is you want to achieve in life, whether that is to become a multimillionaire, run a half-marathon or grow a vegetable garden, it takes motivation, effort and commitment. Nothing boosts your confidence like achieving the goals you have set for yourself. And nothing makes it easier to achieve those goals than believing in yourself and your potential to achieve them.

Remind yourself that you deserve to live a happy and fulfilling life, and before long it will be yours.

The **Fourth Promise** is all about believing you
are going to have a happy and rewarding life.
Whenever you find yourself worrying about the
future, remind yourself to focus on what you do want
and stop worrying about what you don't. Make the
commitment to *believe in your potential* and expect
nothing but the best from your life.

Silence your inner critic

I only welcome thoughts that support and encourage me.

When you listen to your inner dialogue, what do you hear?

Do you hear confidence-nurturing messages and words of encouragement? Does your inner voice rally and cheer you on when you are feeling challenged, providing you with a boost when you need it most? Or perhaps the conversation you are overhearing is an altogether less pleasant one.

At the very start of this book, I shared the story about the little boy who got stuck climbing up a tree and the critical, belittling way his mother spoke to him when he was too afraid to climb down. Most people would agree the best way for her to help him would have been to offer encouraging words and warm-hearted support. Perhaps with this approach the little boy would have found the courage to climb back down – or maybe he still would have needed to be carried but, either way, he would have left the park with his confidence intact and with the courage to try again another day.

I have shared this story with thousands of people, through *The Happiness Code* and through various speaking engagements and seminars. Whenever I tell the story to a live audience, there is always a collective sharp intake of breath as I recount the harsh way this woman spoke to her son: 'Don't be so pathetic.' 'You really are being stupid.' 'What a wimp you are.' 'You really are useless.' I'm sure you felt much the same way as you read those words ...

But how often have you spoken to yourself like that?

How often do you speak to yourself in much the same way as this woman spoke to her son, using words that belittle, berate and undermine your confidence and self-esteem? How often do you call yourself an idiot, stupid or dumb when you make a mistake? How often do you tell yourself you are pathetic, hopeless or a loser when fear gets in your way? How often do you insult yourself, criticise your work or put yourself down because your efforts have been less than perfect?

Never speak to yourself more harshly than you would to a small child.

Whenever you interact with a child you are, in that moment, the guardian of the child's self-esteem. As an adult you are the guardian of *your* self-esteem. You need to guard it vigilantly.

While most people would admit to engaging in self-criticism or negative self-talk some of the time, it is not until they really start paying attention to their internal dialogue that they realise they are engaging in negative self-talk almost all of the time. It's very difficult to feel good about yourself if you are constantly thinking negative thoughts. If you want to maintain a healthy level of confidence and self-belief, you need to put a stop to these messages and take back the ownership of the chat inside your head.

Become your own best friend.

Not everything in life will go as smoothly as you might hope. Making a mistake and wishing you hadn't is part of being human and in no way deserving of the internal flogging far too many people give themselves. If a friend told you a story about how he or she had really messed something up or blown an important opportunity, you would probably find yourself commiserating and then saying whatever you thought your friend needed to hear in order to boost them back up again. This is the approach that you need to take with yourself. Have a moan for a moment, let out your frustration or disappointment and then move into confidence-repair mode.

If you want to build (or rebuild) your confidence and self-esteem you need to silence your inner critic and tell him or her to *ferme la bouche*. (That means *shut up*, but it sounds so much nicer in French!) You wouldn't speak to a friend or lover this way, you know far better than to speak to a child this way and it is time to show yourself the same kindness and respect.

Your inner critic, the voice of your negative thoughts and limiting self-beliefs, sits deep within your subconscious and is your personal enemy number one. Media and lifestyle icon Arianna Huffington describes this voice in a *Huffington Post* article as the 'obnoxious room-mate in your head'. She says:

> Even our worst enemies don't talk about us the way we talk to ourselves … [This voice] feeds on putting us down and strengthening our insecurities and doubts. I wish someone would invent a tape recorder that we could attach to our brains to record everything we tell ourselves. We would realize how important it is to stop this negative self-talk.

Anna's inner critic had a very loud voice. Although she was outwardly a happy and enthusiastic person, on the inside she was being beaten black and blue by the voice inside her head. It seemed that nothing she ever did was good enough, and boy did her inner critic let her know it.

Anna came to one of my workshops with the objective of getting clear about what she wanted from life, but it was very clear to me that unless she silenced the voice in her head the only thing she was going to get was a headache!

Your inner dialogue is based on fiction.
It's time to rewrite the story.

I asked the group to do a simple exercise where they listed their top ten faults. Anna wrote at speed and was the first to finish. Never shy of overachieving, she had added an extra four points to her list too. But when I asked the group to list their top ten positive qualities, Anna's pen was still. When pressed she managed 'I have a nice smile' before putting her pen down in defeat.

Anna wasn't the only woman in the workshop to find the exercise challenging, but as I asked the group to think more creatively with questions like 'What does your best friend like most about you?' 'What is your mother most proud of about you?' and 'How would your children describe you?' she slowly began to build her list.

Once everyone in the group had at least ten things on their list, I asked each person to read their list out loud. As Anna finished reading, her voice caught with emotion. She was truly moved to hear herself described in such glowing terms and couldn't believe how harsh she usually was on herself. Armed with her new set of messages she was ready to silence her inner critic for good.

Your subconscious is very simple. It doesn't evaluate messages, weighing them up for accuracy or usefulness; it just regurgitates the information it has received. What goes in comes out. The problem is, of course, that if the information going in isn't useful, helpful or even accurate, it is still received as fact and filed away to be repeated back to you over time.

Think of a music track set to 'repeat' on your iPod or music player. The same song gets played over and over, the lyrics get stuck in your head and before long you can't think of anything else. That's what your inner critic is like; it repeats the same old track over and over and eventually this thought takes over your consciousness. The result is to virtually brainwash you into thinking that these negative messages are true.

If you fill your thoughts with positive, confidence-building messages, this is what your subconscious will retain and replay. If you fill it with negativity, self-criticism and self-doubt, this is the track you will be stuck with.

Not only does putting yourself down diminish your confidence, but each time you berate, chastise or belittle yourself for making a mistake or for being less than perfect in some way you are also providing your subconscious with more and more negative messages to store and repeat.

If you want to feel like a winner,
you need to learn how to cheer yourself on.

Pay attention to the voice in your head. Listen, not just to the language you use, but also to the tone of voice. Harsh, critical or sarcastic communication has no place in your life, especially when you are the source of it! Do you speak to yourself like a drill sergeant, barking commands and insults and creating an internal environment that oscillates between fear and humiliation? Or is your approach more like that of a cheerleader, singing motivational anthems and chants as you rev your side up to do well in the game? While the drill sergeant's approach may be appropriate when the objective is to break down the individual to ensure that, in times of national crisis, orders are followed collectively and unquestioningly, in the *game of life*, it is the cheerleaders' approach that will help you to feel like a winner.

Not only do you need to stop being negative towards yourself, but what you really want is also for your internal dialogue to be actively positive – cheering you on like a best friend should. The language you use should be warm, encouraging, positive and supportive; the kind of language you would use anytime you were hoping to bring out the best in someone. After all, don't you want to bring

out the best in *you*? When was the last time you
told yourself that you were brilliant, wise, beautiful,
handsome, clever or courageous?

*You are an amazing person, a complex
mix of qualities and characteristics unique
to you. There is nobody else in the world
quite like you.*

You are a good person, you are someone who tries
to do their best and wants to be supportive toward
the people you love. (How do I know this? I feel
completely confident in this description because you
wouldn't have been drawn to this book if being those
things weren't important to you!)

Did you enjoy reading these descriptions, or did
you find yourself feeling uncomfortable and eager
to brush them off with some excuse about why they
don't really apply to you? The answer for far too
many people is they are much more comfortable with

negative descriptions of themselves than they are with positive ones. In the Third Promise I explained why comparing yourself to others and using that as a reason to put yourself down or feel *less than* is counterproductive to your confidence and self-esteem. It is just as destructive to allow your inner critic to be the one leading the downhill charge.

You can't expect to feel good about yourself if you focus on what is bad.

Nobody is perfect. We are all a mix of positive qualities and less-than-ideal ones. Instead of focussing on all that is wrong with you, focus on what is right. Instead of thinking of the mistakes you've made, focus on the things you got right. Instead of highlighting all the things you need to change, shift your attention to all the things you hope will stay the same. Be consciously aware of your positive qualities. Write them down so you can keep your list close to hand

and ready to call on when your confidence needs a boost. When you find yourself engaging in negative self-talk, reviewing this list will literally change the track you have been listening to.

When I suggest this to my clients, I am usually met with resistance. From a young age it is impressed upon us that we mustn't be big-headed or vain, but there is nothing egotistical about knowing your positive qualities. Authentic confidence is never boastful or conceited. It is only when someone is overcompensating for feeling insecure or unsure of themselves in some way that their display of 'confidence' becomes unpleasant or overbearing.

Don't be afraid to be proud of who you are. Authentic confidence is never boastful or conceited.

You don't need to chant your positive qualities out loud, list every single one of them on an internet dating site or rattle them off whenever you meet someone new for the first time, but you do need to know what they are. Having this list at the top of your mind means that any time you find your subconscious moving towards a fictional narrative about any or all of the things that are wrong with you, you can quickly replace those thoughts with facts.

The way you speak to yourself has a huge bearing on how you feel about yourself. You can't expect to feel good when your focus is on everything bad. Negative thoughts lead to negative feelings, which give rise to more negative thoughts, and so the cycle continues.

This applies even if you are not fully committed to the negative messages you are sending your subconscious. If you are undermining, belittling or criticising yourself out of habit in a misguided attempt at humility or in self-deprecating humour, those messages will still stick. Your subconscious will still accept them as fact, and mentally you will file these thoughts away as self-description instead of the fictions that they are. Self-deprecation is only funny in a comedy act. Unless you are on stage, there is nothing to be gained by putting yourself down.

It all begins with your thoughts. How you think determines how you feel, so rather than trying to force yourself to feel differently, challenge yourself to learn to think differently. If you think you are a good person who deserves good things to flow towards them in life, and you regularly reinforce this message through your internal dialogue, you will feel happy, confident and secure. But if you are constantly telling yourself you are useless, hopeless, stupid or dumb, you will feel unsure, insecure and anxious.

The quickest and easiest way to change your thoughts is to use affirmations: positive, personal, present-tense statements that reinforce the beliefs you want to hold about yourself and the things you want to draw into your life. Affirmations take the premise that your subconscious will believe anything it is told and uses it to your advantage. When you use affirmations, you are effectively reforming your thoughts and reprogramming your subconscious.

For an affirmation to be truly effective it needs to be structured in the present tense and express the things you might do, be or have in your ideal life. If you are using affirmations to support you in your goal setting, you will probably focus on *do* and *have*

statements – *I have a promotion, I exercise every day* –
but for the purposes of building your confidence
and boosting your self-belief, *I am* statements will
probably be all that you need: *I am a confident person
who believes in all that I am and all that I can achieve.*

*Change your thoughts and
your feelings will follow.*

The success of an affirmation lies not only in its
language – positive, present-tense and personal – but
also in the repetition. Think about how many times
a day you express a critical, limiting or otherwise
negative statement about yourself. For an affirmation
to be effective you need to repeat it as many if not
more times than the negative messages you send
yourself. The goal is to overpower any negative
thoughts with the strength and frequency of your
new, positive ones.

To get into the habit of saying your affirmations,
follow the rule of threes – repeat the affirmation to

yourself a minimum of three times, three times a day. Within three days, you will notice a fundamental difference in how you feel about yourself. Your thoughts will have influenced your feelings. Keep this up and before long, the power of your thoughts will have changed your world ... or, at the very least, the way you feel about it.

The fastest way to change your life is to change the way you think about it.

Your thoughts inform your feelings, and your feelings are what will determine your actions. Many people misunderstand this process and operate under the assumption that the way they *feel* drives all that they do. 'I felt like ice-cream so I ate it', 'I didn't feel like exercising so I didn't', 'I felt angry so I lost my temper', 'I felt impatient so I snapped' and so on, but it's the way you think about a situation that will determine how you respond to it emotionally.

If there is something you want to do, whether it's achieve a big ambition, break an old habit, form a new one, or simply cross something off your to-do list, the first thing you need to do is make sure you are thinking about it in the right way. Listen in to your internal dialogue. Are you speaking of your objective and your ability to achieve it in a positive way, or is your inner critic already sowing seeds of doubt and telling you that you are likely to fail?

If you want to achieve it,
you need to believe it.

If you have failed at something in the past, don't allow your inner critic to convince you that this is the best you can expect of the future and undermine your success before you even start. Silence your inner critic with clear strong messages about what it is you are going to achieve and why achieving it is important to you.

These strong and positive thoughts will guide your feelings, so that when you are faced with a situation that could lead you astray or allow you to fail, staying on track will feel like the most comfortable and natural option for you. 'I thought about having an ice-cream but decided to go for a walk instead', 'I felt really angry but took a deep breath and decided not to speak until I had calmed down', 'I thought about how frustrated I was and realised that taking it out on the person serving me wouldn't make any difference at all'. Your thoughts inform your feelings and your feelings will guide your actions.

Milo was an interior designer who was down on his luck … or at least he thought he was. Milo's business wasn't growing nearly as fast as he wanted it to and he had been referred to me by a more successful friend.

He was convinced the difference in their circumstances was because his friend was lucky in business and he wasn't. I tried to find a polite way to tell him this was nonsense. For a start, I knew firsthand how hard the friend in question had worked to achieve the level of success she had. I also knew that Milo had been letting a negative perspective stop him from seeing the good fortune and opportunity – the luck – all around him.

I asked Milo to make a list of all the things that would be different in his life if he were a lucky person. Then I asked him to spend the next month acting as if he *was* a lucky person. He was resistant at first and didn't believe that 'pretending' to be lucky was a good use of his time. I was firm and told him that this was what he needed do.

If you want to do something differently, you need to start by thinking about it differently.

At our next coaching session Milo was adamant nothing had changed for him at all. As far as he was concerned it had all been a waste of time. I asked Milo to talk me through his month and I was surprised at what I heard. He had been contacted by a magazine editor who wanted to give her home a makeover but she didn't have much of a budget;

he'd been selected as a finalist in an interior design competition but he hadn't won; and he'd received a referral from a previous client but the job was overseas. In his eyes there had been no money, no prizes and no possibility. What I saw was an editorial opportunity, an accolade and the chance to add 'international' to his bio.

When I shared my re-framing with Milo, he was shocked. Even he could see that he had been showered with opportunities. He went away determined to see himself as lucky, and from that point on keep his eyes open to the good fortune and opportunity all around him.

There is nothing wrong with feeling angry or frustrated if things don't go as well as you had hoped. As unpleasant as it may feel at the time, these are healthy emotions and you shouldn't try to deny or stifle them. What you can do, however, is pay attention to how you express your feelings, both when talking about your experiences to others and, most importantly, to yourself. Make sure you are describing your emotions, instead of demonstrating them. Say 'I am really angry with myself' not 'I am such an idiot'. Instead of 'I am such a fool', try 'I feel embarrassed about the mistake I made'. Instead of cursing at yourself, focus on forgiving yourself.

When things don't go your way, take a deep breath and aim to get over it or let it go as quickly as possible. You don't need to beat yourself up. In fact the only conversation you need to have with yourself is the one where you recap your lessons learned and think about what you will do differently next time.

Don't let your failure in the past
get in the way of your success in the future.

By paying close attention to your inner dialogue, you will be able to catch your inner critic in the act. Instead of allowing your subconscious to sabotage your self-confidence you will be able to intervene and return to healthy, self-esteem boosting thoughts before any real damage can be done.

Changing the way you think takes practice, but while initially you might not be able to control every single thought you have, you can still decide which ones you want to pay attention to.

The **Fifth Promise** is all about protecting your self-esteem from the negative voices inside your head. Instead of berating yourself or putting yourself down, treat yourself like you would your best friend. Make the commitment to *silence your inner critic* and only welcome thoughts that support and encourage you.

Challenge yourself

*I am brave and willing to
step outside of my comfort zone.*

When you think about your life, what does it look like?

Is your life filled with a variety of interesting
people, places and ideas? Or are you stuck in a rut,
doing the same thing over and over without giving
much thought to whether or not you are even
enjoying it?

Your inner confidence and self-belief are like
muscles; you need to exercise them if you want them
to grow stronger and, as with any form of fitness,
you need to keep up your exercise if you want to
maintain the strength and fitness you currently have.

Doing new things, taking on new challenges and stepping outside of your comfort zone are some of the best ways you can build your confidence and boost your self-esteem.

Learn to believe in yourself the way
a child does. Unconditionally.

As a child you were able to do this often, constantly learning new things at school, trying different sports or activities and continually taking on new responsibilities as you matured. As an adult you may find yourself feeling that all the different roles you currently juggle create more than enough challenge, but these challenges are firmly rooted to your day-to-day life. It is the challenges that take you out of your comfort zone, not those focussed on surviving life within it, that will give your confidence a boost.

The reason young children believe they can do anything is because they have not yet learned to doubt themselves. They have unlimited self-belief. Ask a six-year-old what he or she wants to be when they grow up and you'll witness this limitless self-belief firsthand! All their life experience so far has been about learning new things and discovering that over time they can do pretty much anything they set out to do. This is of course true for most, when the challenges faced are learning to crawl, walk, talk, hold a pencil and learn the alphabet.

But as we move through our early years the challenges we are faced with become more complex and the first awareness of our fallibility kicks in. Some of our classmates are better at maths than us, some find it easier to read, some are sportier, funnier, more popular – on the list goes. This continues and deepens in complexity as we mature, until eventually most of us have faced significant disappointments, like failing a test or exam, falling out with a close friend, having our heart broken or missing out on a job we wanted. Just as we are discovering that we are not invincible after all, the time we have available to explore new things according to our own interests and agenda diminishes. Just the other day, my daughter was telling me how much more time for fun she'd had in kindergarten, but that now she was in Grade 2 life was all just 'learning, learning, learning'. Even at the tender age of seven she could sense that the time available to her for doing and learning the things *she wanted to* was decreasing.

Stop saying 'I can't'.
You can ... if you want to.

We enter adulthood with our confidence having taken a few hard knocks. At the same time, many people find they are so busy doing all the things they have to do that they no longer have time to try some of the things they would like to. They are too busy doing the same old thing to try new things. Their confidence is reduced and they are no longer engaged in the kinds of activities that would give it a natural and automatic boost.

If your confidence and self-esteem are not as robust as they once were, the thought of being brave, stepping outside of your comfort zone or trying new things can fill you with fear, anxiety, concern or some other altogether unpleasant feeling.

One of the most important changes you can make in your efforts to become braver is to learn to eliminate 'I can't' from your vocabulary. Every time you say 'I can't', you are making an excuse for how you really feel. 'I can't' can mean many things: 'I don't want to', 'I don't know how to' or 'I am afraid to'. It might mean, 'I'm not available', but it could just as easily mean, 'I *don't want* to be available'. You might say 'I can't go to Zumba', but you might mean 'I think I will feel foolish because I'm not a good dancer'. (Believe me, good dancer or not, you will love it!) You might say, 'I can't go away for the weekend', but you might mean, 'I'm worried I will worry about my children so much I won't enjoy myself'. I'm sure you have a few examples of your own.

I remember a somewhat passionate 'debate' with a very dear friend many years ago. She had young children and I hadn't yet entered that stage of my life. She was explaining all the things she felt she 'can't' do now she had children; no spontaneous drinks after work, no staying up all night reading a good book, no going away for weekends with the girls and so on. I, in a way that I'm sure seemed obtuse to her, kept saying 'why not?' She would try to explain, and I'd attempt to help her find a solution – ask your husband if he can come home early, drink an extra coffee, arrange for your in-laws to help and so on – until the time came for us to agree to disagree and firmly change the subject.

There is no such thing as a good or bad feeling. All that matters is the power you give them.

When you say 'I can't' you are telling your subconscious that this is not possible for you. It was only when I had children of my own that I realised what she was really saying was, 'I don't want to', 'I find it hard to', 'I'm not comfortable with ...' and 'it's too much effort'. When I shared this with her all those years later, she looked surprised and said,

'Of course that's what I meant, what did you think I was saying?' But I, like her subconscious, had thought she genuinely believed she couldn't.

When you challenge yourself, you send a strong message to your subconscious. You are saying, 'I am worth the risk'.

Your feelings are your own and you are 100 per cent entitled to them. There is no such thing as a good or bad feeling; all that matters is the power you give them. Owning up to our thoughts and feelings validates them, and the honesty of articulating the real reason why you don't want to do something is not only liberating, it's confidence-boosting. It is only when you are honest with yourself and, instead of saying 'can't', say what you really mean, that you can then decide if your former 'I can't' is something worth turning into an 'I can'.

As my friend's children got older she realised that some of the limits she had placed upon herself were unnecessary constraints and others were boundaries that protected her values. She has now ditched the former and continues to vigilantly guard the latter.

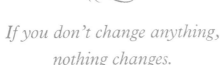

If you don't change anything,
nothing changes.

If you want to boost your confidence and get out of any rut you find yourself in, whether it's social, environmental or behavioural, you need to learn to be brave and make confidence-boosting behaviour a part of your life. When I say this in my workshops, someone invariably tells me that they have far too many responsibilities in their life to be brave. As adults we all have myriad responsibilities we need to consider, but what I am suggesting is courage, not reckless abandon. There is nothing confidence-enhancing about behaving in a destructive or foolish manner. Nor should you be cavalier and risk the things that are good in your life. The kind of bravery

I am talking about involves stepping outside of your comfort zone and committing to a physical activity that previously intimidated you, trying new foods and flavours, mixing up your daily routine, making new friends, doing something that intellectually scares you, going places on your own or saying yes to invitations you would usually turn down.

You don't need to go skydiving to build your self-esteem. Anything that takes you outside of your comfort zone, challenges you or teaches you something new will have the same confidence-boosting effect. When you challenge yourself, you are telling your subconscious that you believe in yourself and that you are willing to back yourself in new circumstances and situations. You are telling your subconscious that you are worth the risk.

Sometimes trying something new isn't as hard as you thought it might be – it might even be surprisingly easy – but, more often that not, as the name suggests, stepping outside of your comfort zone is uncomfortable. If you don't change anything, nothing changes, but if you want to build your confidence and boost your self-esteem, one of the best changes you can make is to give yourself regular challenges. As I always say to my clients, *get comfortable with discomfort.*

Just because the thought of doing something makes you feel nervous, uncomfortable or outright terrified, it doesn't mean you shouldn't do it. Instead of letting your feelings get in your way, be brave. You don't need to expend a lot of time or energy understanding or getting to grips with your fears; when it comes to taking action all you need to do is acknowledge your fears and carry on regardless.

*Don't let your feelings
stand in your way.*

I want to be clear here. I'm talking about the type of uncomfortable feeling you get when facing something different or new. I'm not talking about ignoring an intuition or instinct you might have that something is not right. When you get that feeling you need to pay very close attention and then act on it.

Angela was a single mother who felt there wasn't nearly enough fun in her life. Yes, she had good times with her two boys, whom she adored, but that was 'kid-fun'. What was missing in her life was 'grown-up fun'. Wanting to feel better about her life, Angela enrolled in one of my online workshops and we connected in the support forum.

Angela posted the following question: 'What if the thing you want to do, to step outside of your comfort zone, makes you feel physically sick?' To which I responded, 'Properly nauseated or just good old-fashioned terrified?'

Angela was terrified and she wanted advice on being brave. She'd decided to try one of the things that had always been on her bucket list and had enrolled in a belly-dancing course. As soon as she handed over her credit card details her nerves kicked in. She was worried she would look like a fool, that she would be the oldest in the class, that her belly would wobble more than a belly dancer's should do and that her child-bearing abdominals were so weak she wouldn't be able to move her stomach at all.

I explained to Angela that just because something makes you feel nervous doesn't mean you need to let your nerves get in the way. Simply acknowledge your discomfort and then carry on regardless. I gave her the same advice I give my children when they are feeling nervous about something. I told Angela to say to her nerves, 'Hello nerves, I can hear you loud and clear, but you'll have to excuse me, I've got things I need to do.'

Angela realised that she didn't need to *get over* her nerves to enjoy her belly-dancing class; she could simply invite them along for the ride.

People often ask me how you can tell the difference between an emotive fear, the kind that is driven by the feelings you have about stepping outside of your comfort zone, and an instinctive or intuitive fear, the kind that is warning you something is really wrong. My answer is to look for the feeling in your body. More often than not, you will experience your emotive fears, the kind that ultimately are a good sign, in your stomach and occasionally rising up to your chest (though if you do try sky-diving, you may well feel it all the way up to your ears!). The point is that healthy fears have a very specific anchor point in your body. They begin in your stomach, hence the expressions 'feeling sick to your stomach' and 'I felt it in the pit of my stomach', and expand through your body from there.

You don't need to go into battle with your fears. They don't need to be defeated. You just need to own up to them and then let them go.

An intuitive or instinctive fear will be felt at a cellular level; it's as if every cell in your body is trying to warn you that something is not right. I often describe these intuitive feelings as something I could feel 'right down to my fingertips'. When you experience fear in this way, you should pay close attention to it and act on it accordingly. Instinctive or intuitive fear is serious. It is your subconscious warning you of impending danger, and whether that danger is physical, mental or emotional you want to get away from it as fast as you can. What you don't want to do, however, is give every fear you have this level of power. The fact is, most of the fears you experience will be emotive and driven by your feelings. Instead of giving in to these fears, simply acknowledge them and move on.

Be brave. Face your fears and then carry on regardless.

I like to pretend that I'm fearless, but of course I'm not. However whenever I find myself experiencing fear my goal is to reduce its power by moving through it. By carrying on regardless. You don't need to go into battle with your fears. They don't need to be defeated. But you do need to own up to them. When you try to ignore your fears, you fuel the power they have over you.

Just as you shouldn't ignore your fears, you also shouldn't judge them, label them or belittle and berate yourself for having them. Negativity will only serve to fuel your fears further as your self-esteem takes a beating and your fear begins to present itself as reality. When I find myself experiencing an emotive fear, I always acknowledge it with emotionally neutral language. Owning up to your fears reduces their power immediately.

When I discover a fear, I say to myself, 'I am experiencing fear, how interesting'; 'I'm feeling intimidated by this business meeting. Isn't that interesting.' It is not good. It is not bad. It is simply cause for curiosity. I find this neutral language disempowers my fears. They are not good or bad and I am not a better or worse person for having them. They are simply an interesting development. I don't let them stop me and always remind myself I can always go back and explore them further if and when I have the time … and the inclination.

Learning how to be assertive, how to state your case firmly but not aggressively, is one of the most important confidence-boosting skills you can develop. But for many people, women in particular, it is also one of the hardest. Learning to be assertive plays into many people's fears about not being liked, about being seen as rude or disagreeable or simply not being 'nice'. Asking for what you want, politely but firmly, doesn't make you rude or disagreeable, it makes you someone with a clear understanding of what they want or need. And nice – well, nice is definitely overrated as a virtue when, really, it is often shorthand for 'they don't rock the boat or have opinions or ideas of their own'.

When you don't stand up for yourself, whether that is not letting the waiter know your meal has been served cold, not asking for what you need in a relationship or allowing someone to treat you disrespectfully, you are complicit in the erosion of your self-esteem. Being meek doesn't serve you. All staying quiet does is tell your subconscious that your views have no value and your needs are not important. It's only a very short journey from this point for your subconscious to conclude that *you* don't hold any value and *you* are not important.

The first time you are assertive, it can be quite a surprise to find that the world doesn't end. Don't get me wrong, the other party might not like what you have to say. But it won't kill them to hear it. What you learn by being assertive is that you can survive someone being unhappy with you and what you've had to say. It might not be pleasant and you might not enjoy it, but those feelings will quickly pass and you will feel much, much better for it. Of course the other benefit is you also stand a much better chance of getting your wants or needs met.

One of the bravest things you can do
is stand up for yourself
and what you believe in.

I met Brian when he attended one of my breakout sessions, on how to get what you want from life, at the annual conference for his industry. The topic of how and when to communicate assertively came up.

Unlike a lot of women who worry they will be seen as rude if they are assertive, Brian feared he would be seen as aggressive if he asked for what he wanted in such a precise way.

I explained that true assertive behaviour is neither aggressive nor rude, but firm and clear. I asked Brian to recount a time when he hadn't asked for what he wanted or needed because he was worried he would be seen as aggressive and how it had turned out for him.

Brian told the story of a date he'd been on where he'd been 'forced to eat salad' when the waitress had delivered a bacon and avocado *salad* instead of a bacon and avocado *sandwich*. His date had noticed the error and pointed out that his meal wasn't what he'd ordered. She encouraged him to send the meal back, but in his desire to avoid being seen as aggressive he said it would be fine and he would eat it anyway.

Don't be afraid to ask for what you need. You deserve it.

Except he didn't. He picked at the leaves and tried to dig out the bacon. His date noticed and once again suggested he send back his meal. Again he declined but, feeling embarrassed, his voice sounded firmer than he intended. His date was taken aback by his tone and their meal went downhill from there. Needless to say, there wasn't a second date.

Listening to Brian's story I asked if he could see that by not being assertive and communicating his needs in a calm but firm way, he had bottled up his frustration only to have it blurt out in an inappropriate way.

Brian couldn't help but chuckle when he thought it all through. All this time he had been blaming the salad for the bad end to his date when the responsibility was his all along. It wasn't the lettuce leaves that had done anything wrong!

Standing up for yourself, asking for what you want, expressing your views or articulating your dissatisfaction does not make you a bad person. It makes you an assertive person. Any discomfort you feel when being assertive will be far outweighed by the growth in your self-esteem.

I gave a radio interview recently and the topic of other people's opinions came up. I casually mentioned that I am not concerned with other people's opinions of me. One of the program hosts said incredulously, 'Are you really telling me that you don't care what people think of you?' As I explained to her, of course I would prefer it if everyone I met liked me – that would be the most pleasant way to travel through life – but if you ask me if I need that or if it is important to me, it is not. There are a few people whose views of me really do matter: my husband, children, close family and a few close friends. If I am looking for counsel, these are the people I will call on and they are the same people I can rely on to be honest with me and call me out if I am getting something wrong. But as for everyone else, I really can't invest my energy in what their thoughts about me are. The radio announcer told me I was brave. It may be brave but, as I explained to her, it was also very sensible.

Decide whose opinion matters and stop worrying about everyone else.

You can't keep everybody happy all of the time. So don't try. As one of my early mentors, Matt Church, international speaker and founder of Thought Leaders™, is fond of saying, '*Some will, some won't, so what?*' Decide whose opinion really does matter to you and then bravely (and sensibly) forget about the rest.

At some point in your life, you probably have, and will again be, faced with a difficult situation, moral dilemma or some other conflicting circumstance. When this happens you will usually have a number of options for handling the situation, the most common of which are the chance to do the right thing and the option of doing the easy thing.

Situations like these can be incredibly difficult, but hiding away or wheedling out of the tough decision or conversation won't do your self-esteem any good. The more you try to 'sit' on a situation, hope it will go away or sweep it under the carpet, the more it will fester. Not only is this deeply unpleasant, but it also actively erodes your self-esteem. Fortune favours the bold, or so the saying goes, but not only are the brave rewarded financially – they are also rewarded in self-confidence. As bad as it might feel in the moment, doing something tough, when you know it is the right thing to do, will have a lasting effect on your self-esteem.

One of the kindest things you can do for yourself is actively invest your energy in building your self-esteem. For the most part, while a little daunting, many of the challenges you give yourself will have the potential to end up being fun, life-enhancing changes.

But even when the situation is a far more difficult one, your self-esteem will reward you for having the courage to face it.

*When you do the right thing,
regardless of how you feel while doing it,
you will always feel good for having done it.*

Being brave and stepping out of your comfort zone is an important component in feeling good about who you are and the life you live. Being brave can be tough in the short term, but it is much, much better for you in the long term.

The **Sixth Promise** is all about actively building up your confidence. Decide to be brave and step outside of your comfort zone. Try new things and tell your subconscious that you are worth the risk. Make the commitment to *challenge yourself* and watch your confidence level soar.

Stop making excuses

*I take full responsibility for
who I am and the life I lead.*

Are you honest with yourself about who you are and
the life you live?

Are you aware of what is working well in your life,
clear about what you would like to change and sure of
the steps you need to take? Or do you keep your head
in the sand, avoiding your reality, hoping that one day
things will somehow change all on their own?

It's time for some tough love!

While I'm not a fan of the sentiment 'you have to
be cruel to be kind', I do believe sometimes you need
to be firm to be kind. You know those times when

someone you love is heading off track and, as hard
as it is, you need to sit them down and have *the chat*?
Well, sometimes you need to be able to do that for
yourself. While you might only butt in on a friend's
life when an issue becomes serious, when it comes
to your own life, you are probably better off having a
firm chat sooner rather than later.

You don't need to be cruel to be kind,
but you do need to be honest.

Have you ever found yourself thinking about
something you need or want to do, only to find
yourself preparing the excuse you are going to give
for not getting it done before you even get started?
When you see it written down like that, it sounds like
crazy behaviour, but it really is very common. In fact,
every time you say 'I'll try …' or 'yeah, but …' you
are preparing your personal get-out clause. I'm sure
if you think back even just over the last week, you
will be able to come up with an occasion when you

said you were going to try to do something 'but …' and had your excuse for not doing it already in place before you got properly started.

Be realistic about what you intend to do and honest about what you are able to do.

It might not seem important at the time, but each time you make an excuse for yourself you are undermining your self-belief. It's like saying to yourself, 'I never really believed I could', 'I don't really think I can' or 'It doesn't matter if I do'. Making excuses left, right and centre for the little things you've said you'd do and haven't done will only eat away at your confidence. Instead, learn to be more honest with yourself about what you do and don't want to do, what you are and aren't likely to get done, and what is realistic and what is impossible.

In my workshops one of the most common criticisms I hear people make about themselves is that they are no good at time management; that they need to work out how to get more done if they are going to achieve their potential. But the secret to time management isn't miraculously being able to do more; it is starting to get serious about doing less. Instead of filling your to-do list with a million things, starting a hundred of them, finishing one or two and feeling like a failure, focus on the two or three important things you need to do, get those done and feel like a success.

In my first book, *Your Best Life*, I wrote about managing your time and getting more out of your day. While acquiring the fundamental skills of organisation and prioritisation will stand you in good stead in life, when it comes to preserving and building your confidence, what matters is not how much you can or can't do, but that you keep the commitments that you make about what you *are* going to do. Pay just as much attention to the little commitments you make. Although the outcomes themselves might not be as significant, the message you send your subconscious, about whether or not you are the kind of person who keeps their commitments, is significant. Becoming the kind of person who does what they say they are going to do will give your confidence a huge boost.

Although the phrase *under promise, over deliver*
became popular through its use in business, there is a
lot to be gained from applying it in your everyday life.
What this expression really means is, say you're going
to do less than you think you can do and then do a
little bit more. This approach is the exact opposite
of what most people do, which is to attempt to do
everything, struggle to get any of it done properly and
then end up feeling bad about what they haven't done.

*When you commit to yourself and
your intentions, the message you send
yourself is 'I am worth this effort'.*

At first it can feel uncomfortable or even
counterintuitive to offer to do less. But as you succeed
at keeping your commitments the benefits to your
confidence and self-belief will far outweigh any short-
term discomfort at no longer being the kind of person
who attempts to do it all.

Being honest with yourself is incredibly empowering. While it might be easier, and in the short term more pleasant, to deceive yourself, taking responsibility for your life is liberating. It allows you to fully evaluate what is working and what isn't, what you enjoy and what you don't, and what needs to change and what you would like to stay exactly the same.

It is easy to look at someone else's life from afar and think that it is perfect. But just as no individual can ever be perfect, nobody's life will ever be perfect either. What you are seeing, when you look at a life that fills you with inspiration, envy or possibly a mix of both, is often the result of the effort and commitment that person is making toward the goal of living their best life.

This is definitely true for me. I live a good life. It's not perfect, but I really do love it. I have a job I love, but I have left many jobs I didn't enjoy on the path to getting to where I am today. I have a loving and committed relationship with my husband, but we chose each other very carefully and have continued to work on our relationship and resolve our issues as and when they arise, rather than leaving them to fester. I enjoy good health, some of which I am sure is genetic, but much of which is a result of the choices I make about how I live my life. I eat healthily, drink alcohol only in moderation, exercise regularly and make time to relax.

Taking responsibility for your life is liberating.

Fleur had been given the opportunity to be the acting editor of a home decorating magazine while her boss was on maternity leave. Not only did Fleur covet her boss's job on a professional level, but on a personal level she had always been envious of the glamour associated with the editor's role: hosting fancy lunches for advertisers, receiving a home decorating allowance, and planning and selecting the image to be used on the cover.

Fleur wasn't worried about the increase in her responsibilities. From her perspective the editor's role was largely oversight and approval … and a lot of lunches. It was she and her colleagues who worked their butts off to get each month's issue ready for print. Or so she thought.

Nobody's life is perfect.
What looks like perfection from afar is
usually the result of
hard work and commitment.

Stepping into her boss's role was quite an eye-opener for Fleur. It wasn't nearly as easy as she thought it was going to be. Although she wasn't as hands-on in the magazine creation as she had been in her previous role, her day was filled with a lot of meetings, and there were so many people she needed to keep happy. The advertisers wanted to know their product would be profiled, the publisher wanted her to change the cover, her team wanted her to approve their holidays, and those lunches … well they really were hard work after all.

Fleur quickly came to realise it wasn't that the editor's job had been easy – it was that her boss had *made it look easy* because she was so confident and competent at what she did. Fleur continued to work hard and learn as much as she could, and by the time her boss returned to work she had begun to make it look a little easier too.

None of this is rocket science and it certainly doesn't make me any better than the next person. What it does illustrate, however, is that a life that looks good from the outside – great job, good relationship, healthy body and happy heart – is not just luck. It is the result of being truly honest with yourself about what you want and need in your life and then applying your full commitment to making this your reality.

Of course there are still many things about my life I want to change and improve. Goals I want to achieve, bad habits I want to conquer and new hurdles I will have to learn to leap over. But it is only by taking full responsibility for who you are and the life you are living that *your best life* can become your reality.

Think again about that person whose life you have admired or envied and take a moment to consider the choices they have made and the commitments they have upheld to get their life into the shape it is in. Now take a minute to consider your own life. Are you living your best life or at the very least working towards it, or are you just getting by, trudging from one day to the next? Do you remind yourself that the life you are living right now is the only chance you will get to be happy and fulfilled? Are you making the most of this gift or are you frittering it away?

*Decide to live your best life
and then do whatever you need to do
to make it happen.*

I have been blessed to have lived a life that has been largely free of trauma and suffering. As I write this though, a list of things that have been tough rush to the front of my mind. I have been the victim of heinous bullying, not just as a child, but also early on in my career. I survived a car accident that left me with an injury that took nearly ten years to heal and

I have suffered a number of miscarriages, including one where my life was at risk. During these most challenging times in my life I made the conscious decision not to be an unhappy person, but a happy person who was going through a difficult time.

Don't let your past define your future.

We cannot choose our childhoods, but we can choose the way we live our adult lives. We have no say in the parents we are born to or many of the myriad events God/the universe/life throws in our path. What we can do, however, is decide how we are going to experience these events and whether we will allow them to define our lives or simply reinforce our strength and character.

At any point you can reclaim your narrative and decide how you want the story of your future to be told. You may not have been blessed with a happy childhood, you may have suffered illness and tragedy far greater than I could or would want to imagine, but you still have a choice as to what you do with those experiences. They can be your version of 'that which doesn't break you makes you stronger' or you can allow them to become your excuses for not being all that you have the potential to be and living the best life you possibly can.

At any point you can decide how you want the story of your future to be told.

If you choose to see yourself as a victim of your past, you will render yourself powerless to create your future. Whenever you make the choice to fully embrace your life, regardless of what you have been dealt in the past, your confidence will blossom.

Monica Lewinsky wrote bravely for *Vanity Fair* magazine about what it was like to be at the centre of one of the biggest political scandals of the last century.

She explained how, at the age of forty, she was no longer prepared to let her past define her future. In this article she explained how she was taking responsibility for her future: 'I've decided, finally, to stick my head above the parapet so that I can take back my narrative and give a purpose to my past.'

If the life you are living feels any less than it could be, as well as assessing what is missing you need to understand *why* it is missing. All too often, people fall into the trap of moaning about the things that are wrong with their life without stopping to think not only about what they can do to start making it right, but also how and why things turned out the way they did in the first place.

Taking responsibility is completely different to blaming yourself. When you blame yourself, you take on *all* of the responsibility for a situation regardless of where the true ownership lies. When you blame yourself you lose the true perspective of a situation and invite confidence-crushing feelings like shame, humiliation and guilt. Taking responsibility has the opposite effect on your self-esteem. It's about saying 'I had a role in this, and whether I was conscious of it or not at the time, I must now take my share of ownership for how the situation turned out'. Once you are aware of your responsibility – to a situation, to a person or to yourself – you are able to calmly evaluate your options for recourse and confidently plan the next steps you want to take.

Taking responsibility is about acting with courage and integrity.

If the situation or circumstance includes other people, whether it's a falling out with a friend, a costly mistake at work or an indiscretion between lovers, taking responsibility is about acting with courage and integrity. However, taking responsibility for situations that affect you and you alone is just as important and in many cases harder to do; there are no relationships or reputations to protect, no-one will ever know if you did in fact do the right thing by yourself, no-one will ever know if the person you lied to or cheated on was yourself. But unless you are truly honest with yourself, you will find it very hard to move forward into the future you deserve.

The range of things you may need to take some or all the responsibility for is wide and isn't limited to the purely negative. If you stay up late watching television you need to take responsibility for how tired you will feel in the morning. If you overindulge in your favourite foods you need to take responsibility for your weight gain. If you neglect your relationships, you need to take a share of the responsibility for their potential demise. If you accept a promotion at work you need to take some responsibility for the increase to your workload or stress level. If you start a family you need to take responsibility for the change in your level of personal or social freedom.

It is only by taking responsibility for our circumstances or actions that we are able to clearly evaluate the choices that led us to this point in our life and the new decisions that will need to be made if you are to move toward an even better future.

Sometimes, knowing what changes you want and need to make in your life is not enough to make you actually do them. There is an expression I find very insightful: 'people do what works'. Essentially this means that on some level, even if it is a subconscious one, your behaviour is serving a need or desire.

The theory is, if you genuinely and authentically want to make a change, then you will have all the motivation you need to do it. Even if you are finding it hard to source your motivation it is because in some part of your life, it actually serves you better not to make that change. Whenever something is not working for you in one part of your life, it is because it is working for you in some other way. It is this *silent benefit* that is stopping you from moving forward in the way you would like.

For example, if you keep saying you want to lose weight, but can't commit to the diet and exercise plan required to make it happen, ask yourself, in what way does being overweight work for you? Perhaps it helps you to avoid attention and fly under the radar; maybe being overweight serves as an excuse for why your life isn't 'perfect'; or could it be that your weight acts as a blanket, protecting you from unwanted attention from the opposite sex? People do what works.

When I first heard Adrian tell his story, I was moved to tears. He had been an audience member at a keynote speech I made. When my presentation moved on to the subject of goal-setting, I asked the audience if anyone had a story about a goal they had failed to achieve until they found the right motivation. My assistant passed the microphone to a trim, fit forty-something man who stood up and said, 'Hi, I'm Adrian and I'm half the man I used to be.' Like the rest of the audience, I was a little confused at first and wondered where his story was going …

You need to be honest with yourself if you want to create the future you deserve.

Adrian went on to explain that for most of his life he had struggled with his weight. He had trimmed down a little just before he got married but by the time his son came along, the sleepless nights had given him the excuse he needed to stop exercising and the all-round exhaustion zapped him of his motivation to make healthy choices with his food. Adrian knew he was becoming seriously unhealthy, but try as he might he just couldn't stick to a weight loss plan. He'd lose a few kilos and then gain them back, lose them again, only to regain in double. His weight continued to balloon, and by the time his son started school he was 24 stone or 152 kg.

When your desire for change is authentic, you will have all the motivation you need.

Everything changed for Adrian when he went to cheer his son on at his first school sports carnival. At the end of the children's races the headmistress announced the parents' race. First up would be the dads. Adrian took a step back and hoped to blend into the crowd, but there was no hiding. He said he thought his heart would break when he had to tell his son that no, he wouldn't be running in the race. In his innocence his son couldn't understand why his dad didn't want to run and began pleading with him. But Adrian couldn't run. He could barely walk around the block without needing to sit down, and running definitely wasn't an option.

There wasn't a dry eye in the audience when Adrian explained how ashamed he had felt in that moment. He promised himself that the following year he would run in the dad's race and made the commitment then and there to become the kind of dad his son could be proud of. Not because he was fat or thin, but because when he set himself a goal, he didn't give up until he achieved it.

If you can't find your motivation, you need to examine *all* the thoughts and feelings you have on the subject until you can identify the point that is driving you *away* from your goals, not closer to them. Your missing motivation may be caused by any number of reasons, but the most common ones are fear-based. Every change in life will have both good and not-so-great aspects, and it is perfectly natural as you make these changes to feel uncomfortable about some of the potential impact. Instead of allowing your hesitance to eat away at your confidence and make you slip further and further away from your goal, take the time to explore what is really holding you back. Once you identify the cause of your missing motivation, and take responsibility for it, you are free to decide exactly how you want to progress.

One of the most common reasons people don't have what they think they want in life is that they don't really want it. While this sounds elementary, unless you explore why you are having a hard time maintaining your commitment you may not uncover this fundamental truth. People often confuse their dreams with their fantasies. A fantasy is something you enjoy thinking about, but a dream is something you are actually willing to do something about. You may have a fantasy about a certain career, weight, home or lifestyle but for as long as it is a fantasy you will never make any tangible progress towards it. And that is okay … as long as you are clear that a fantasy is all it is.

Don't confuse your dreams and your fantasies. A fantasy is something you enjoy thinking about. A dream is something you are willing to do something about.

Things start to go wrong for your confidence and self-belief when you mistake your fantasies for goals and then criticise or berate yourself for not achieving them. Just because you enjoy thinking about something, doesn't mean you have to have it, or have it right now, in your life. Your fantasy might be something you would like to work toward at a different stage in your life or something deep in your heart you know you are never going to work toward because the compromises or sacrifices are too great, because it conflicts with your values or because you are really only interested in part of the picture, not the whole picture. Instead of feeling bad for not making progress toward your fantasies, accept them for what they are, enjoy thinking about them – but save your energy for making the things you really do want in your life your reality.

The **Seventh Promise** is all about taking responsibility for who you are and the life you live. Don't let fear get in your way and remember that nobody else's life is perfect either. Make the commitment to *stop making excuses* and make *your best life* your reality.

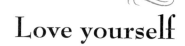

Love yourself

*I always treat myself with
love and respect.*

How well do you treat yourself?

Do you prioritise your happiness and make sure
your needs are met, knowing that the better you take
care of yourself, the better you are able to take care of
everyone else in your life? Or have you neglected your
wants and needs for so long they no longer make it
onto your to-do list at all?

It sounds very simple, but respecting your needs
is one of the most important things you can do for
your confidence and self-esteem. When you don't
respect your needs, you send a very clear message

to your subconscious that says, 'I'm not worth it' or 'I don't matter'.

The better you take care of yourself,
the better you are able to take care of
the other important people in your life.

If you want to feel good about yourself, you need to learn to put taking care of yourself at the top of your list, not at the bottom. You know how the safety announcement on an aeroplane instructs you to put on your own oxygen mask before assisting others? Well, you need to apply that advice to the rest of your life. Whenever I explain this concept to my clients, the first thing they do is give me a list of all the other people they need to take care of or keep happy: children, partners, bosses, colleagues, parents, in-laws, siblings, and on the list goes. I fully agree that any or all of the people on this list may have wants or needs that you are best placed to meet, but unless this person is actually your dependant or child you don't need to put your needs last in order to meet theirs.

If you have children, I agree you must put their fundamental needs ahead of your own. You absolutely should prioritise their food, water and shelter above your own. But all too often I see people, especially women, allow not just their children's needs, but their wants, whims and desires to all but consume them, leaving them far too depleted to do anything for themselves.

I see the same problem with some people who have allowed their work to take over the rest of their life. They cancel social commitments at the last minute, eat unhealthily and exercise rarely and only leave the office to sleep. Although they might believe they are prioritising their desire for career success, when the cost is the rest of your life, this is not success at all.

Prioritising your own needs doesn't make you selfish; it makes you 'self-ist'. It makes you smart. Selfish people put themself first in a way that is detrimental to others. A self-ist person simply acknowledges their needs and makes them a priority. Being self-ist and prioritising your needs is a healthy way to be.

If you want to feel good about yourself, you need to make taking care of yourself a priority. This doesn't just mean getting your basic needs met, but also making sure you make the time to maintain your mental, emotional and physical health.

Prioritising your needs doesn't make you selfish, it makes you self-ist.

Send your subconscious a very clear message about how much you value your life by eating well, exercising regularly and enjoying alcohol only in moderation. Invest in your longevity by going for check-ups regularly and if something is concerning you, get it checked sooner rather than later. Your health is of vital importance and yet so often people forget to prioritise the one thing that gives them the best chance of enjoying a long, happy and healthy life. Their life.

Your mental and emotional wellbeing are just as important as your physical wellbeing. Learn to ask for

help when you need it, either from your friends and
family or, if the need arises, a trained professional.

Asking for help is a sign of strength,
not weakness.

But before you can acknowledge your wants and
needs, you need to know what they are. And in order
to know what they are you need to have taken the time
to consider them. If you want to feel good about who
you are and the life you live, you need to make time
to think about what kind of life you want to be living;
what your values, hopes and dreams are. It is only
when you know what matters to you and what you are
seeking that you are able to set priorities and put in
place boundaries to make this your reality.

Although I am very ambitious in my career, I am
also ambitious for the rest of my life. I am clear about
my values for family and my relationship, and in my
personal hierarchy they sit at the top. What this means
for me is that although I prioritise my own needs,

I don't put my wants first. After my fundamental needs have been met, I prioritise my family and my relationship ahead of my career. In our home, no one person takes priority over another. I make the best decisions I can for us as a family, then I make the best decisions for my husband and me as a couple, and then I do what is best for me personally. Make no mistake, I am not putting myself last; I'm putting myself third.

Focus on your values and
let everything else fall into place.

This description is not meant to be prescriptive. It's just what works for me and aligns with my values. If you want to feel good about yourself and your life, you need to know what your values are, the things that matter most to you. Once you know the answer to this, you are able to confidently set your priorities and know you are doing the right things for you.

If you want to feel good about yourself and your life you need to make sure you are living the life you want to be living. I don't mean living the perfect life. You should know by now that doesn't exist. But the life you want to be living or at the very least striving toward needs to be *your best life*.

You are the only one who can determine what the best life for *you* is. You need to be honest with yourself, both about your goals, hopes and dreams, as well as how you feel about the way you are travelling through life right now. If there are things you need to change about the way you are living your life, make a plan to change them. Be realistic in your planning. Rome wasn't built in a day and your best life won't be created overnight. Ask yourself, 'What can I do that will take me 10 per cent closer to a life that is my best life?' Put those changes in place and, when this starts to feel comfortable and natural to you, you can look at other ways to move your life closer to the one you really want to be living.

The most important thing to remember as you plan to improve your life is to be grateful for all the things that are already in it. Reminding your subconscious how rich and full your life already is will go a long way to giving you the confidence you need to make your life even better.

Gratitude for what you have is one of the greatest gifts you can give yourself.

Once upon a time, when our culture was generally more religious, children were taught to pray before they went to sleep at night. Although I am not religious myself, I see this as one of the great casualties of our modern secular life. Those bedtime prayers were a chance to express your gratitude, express your hopes and set your intentions: *thank you for … please take care of … help me to be …*

Regardless of your own religious preferences you can gain enormously by bringing a version of the nightly prayer back into your life. At the end of each day, before you go to sleep, think of all that you are thankful for or appreciative of in your life and express your gratitude. Next acknowledge your hopes and dreams for your life and finally set your intentions for the following day. If you add this simple ritual to your nightly routine, making it the last thing you think about each night, you will start the following day filled with contentment and confidence.

*End each day with gratitude for today
and goodwill toward tomorrow.*

Love yourself unconditionally. If you want to feel good about yourself, you need to learn to forgive yourself and see that, while you may have made mistakes, you are still a good person and you are still worthy of love and respect.

So many people go through life harbouring grudges against themselves. You are not perfect. You will get things wrong and when you do, you need to forgive yourself and move on. Holding on to negative feelings about something you have done or failed to do will only eat away at your self-esteem. Sometimes you will be able to do something to put things right, and other times there will be nothing you can do to make it right. When you make a mistake or get something wrong, there is nothing to be gained by feeling ashamed. Remind yourself that there is nothing you could have done that is so bad it has never been done before. While that doesn't make your mistake any better, it does put your failings or mistakes into context.

Learn to love yourself unconditionally.

I spoke earlier about how I moved to Sydney just after my 20th birthday and moved in with a man I had met when I had only been there a few weeks. What I didn't say was that I had left my then-boyfriend behind in Perth. This guy was truly lovely and had I met him when I was a bit older ours may have been a very different future. But I was only twenty and I was infatuated with my new life and this new man and, not being someone who wanted a boyfriend on each coast, I ended things. I broke his heart. He was very clear about this.

Although I felt bad to have so badly hurt someone
I cared about, in those heady first few months I was
so caught up in my new relationship I didn't dwell
on it. Eventually the lovely guy moved on and my
new relationship began to show the kind of cracks
that usually befall relationships built on lust and
infatuation, not common values and shared hopes
and dreams. But I soldiered on. I was determined
that, having caused someone so much hurt and pain,
I would make this new relationship work; that it
would be an insult to my former love if I didn't. The
cracks became chasms and I became unhappier. But I
wouldn't give up.

Although I wasn't conscious of it at the time,
sticking with this disastrous relationship was a form
of penance for all the hurt I had caused. Eventually,
after a particularly ugly argument, I called my mother
in tears. Somewhere in my outpouring I talked about
how guilty I felt for the hurt I was responsible for
and how I needed to stick with this relationship to
justify the pain I had caused. Now, anyone who has
read my other books knows just how wise my mother
can be, and this occasion was no different. She said,
'Someone who commits a heinous crime might only

get a three- to four-year sentence. How long are you planning to punish yourself for this supposed crime you have committed?'

Forgive yourself for what you have done or have failed to do.

It took these wise words for me to be able to see what I had been doing and to realise that I needed to forgive myself for the 'crime' of trying to live my life and doing what had seemed right for me at the time.

A short time later I left Sydney for London and left my relationship and my guilt behind. I never looked back.

As well as learning to respect yourself, you need to learn to expect respect from the other people in your life. Whether it is a friend, family member, partner, colleague or your child, the behaviour you accept from other people lets them know how much you value yourself and how much they in turn need to value you.

If you allow people to speak to you rudely, aggressively, dismissively or patronisingly, not only are they disrespecting you, but in accepting their behaviour you are also disrespecting yourself. You are not respecting yourself if you accept dishonesty, tolerate bullying or put up with being pushed around, whether it is at work or in your personal life.

My client Eric was the first to admit that he had messed up his marriage. He had been foolish and had an affair with his secretary, and what had felt exciting at the time turned out to be one of the biggest mistakes he would ever make.

Eric was now an 'every-other-weekend dad', and he hated not being there for his daughter on a day-to-day basis. He promised to make up for failing in his marriage by being the best dad his daughter could hope to have.

When his daughter had been much younger it had been easy to show his love in the things they did together: days out exploring the city, ice-cream in the park and breakfast in bed with a movie in the morning. Eric's daughter had adored him and he had felt he was making good on his promise. But lately something had changed. His daughter didn't delight in his company in the same way, everything he did was *so embarrassing* and there was nothing cool about any of the suggestions he had for their time together. What was worse, she had started to change the way she spoke to him and was now regularly dismissive and rude.

While Eric could accept some of these changes as 'normal teenage behaviour' he wasn't willing to brush it all under the carpet and hope that it would go away. He signed up for one of my online courses and began to examine his options.

Stand up for yourself and teach people how you want to be treated.

Although Eric had failed his wife, he knew he hadn't failed his daughter. He really was the best dad he could be and it was now time to put some boundaries in place, to help his daughter become the best daughter she could be and not the sullen, sulky teenager she was at risk of becoming.

Eric was willing to redefine some of the parameters of their relationship. As sad as it made him, he could see that the days when 'hanging out with Dad' was the most exciting thing in the world had probably come to an end and it was time to allow his daughter more freedom to choose how they spent their time.

At the same time, Eric had a frank and honest conversation with his daughter about how her behaviour made him feel. He reassured her he loved her but insisted that her behaviour toward him needed to change if they were to continue to have a good father-and-daughter relationship.

For her part, while his daughter knew that her behaviour had been less than ideal, in the egocentricity of her youth, how her behaviour made her dad feel hadn't really occurred to her. Now that he had spelled it out, there was no denying it. She promised to make more of an effort and, although she was still very much a 'normal teenager', their relationship once again found an even keel.

When someone does something you don't like, that makes you feel uncomfortable or is unacceptable to you in some other way, you need to tell them what they are doing is wrong and that you need them to stop.

While standing up for yourself in this way can be uncomfortable, the confidence boost you will get from respecting yourself will make you feel ten feet tall.

If you want to be respected, you need to ask for what you want and explain exactly what you need.

You may also need to ask for the respect you deserve in your personal relationships. The friend who never pays their share of the bill, the partner who doesn't do their share at home, the teenager who treats your home like a hotel. Love and respect don't always go hand in hand. In fact it is often the people you love and who love you who take your relationship for granted, and forget to show you respect. When this happens, speak up. Don't allow their behaviour to become a repetitive pattern. Instead tell them how their behaviour is making you feel using simple, non-emotive language. Try following the 'when you

… I feel … and what I need is …' model, for example: 'When you are late without warning me, I feel like my time isn't important to you, and what I need is for you to be on time or let me know well in advance that you are not going to be.' Simple, non-emotive language that makes it very clear to the listener exactly how they can remedy the situation.

One of the most important ways you can value yourself is by making sure your relationships are healthy ones. While I would never judge someone's romantic or sexual choices, what I can't stand to watch is someone I care for entering or maintaining a relationship where they are not being fully respected. There is nothing modern or liberated about being treated disrespectfully, and a lot of what is dressed up as freedom is just that.

Tamara was a modern, independent, professional woman. Ambitious, well dressed and successful, she knew she didn't need a man to be happy and she hadn't had a serious relationship in years. Unless you counted this thing she had with her colleague Matt.

Tamara told herself it didn't matter that he was married; she was single, which meant that she wasn't the one doing anything wrong. But while she might not have been doing anything wrong according to her personal moral code, Tamara was definitely doing the wrong thing for her confidence and self-esteem.

Tamara really didn't want Matt to leave his wife, but her confidence was being eaten away by the realisation that he didn't want her enough to want to. She said she wasn't committed to Matt, but she didn't see any other men. He said he didn't want a commitment to Tamara and he continued to see a number of other women. She lied to her friends so that she could make sure she was available for him when he called. He lied to her and said he would call and then didn't.

Confidence comes from within.
You can't find it in the eyes of someone else.

When Tamara attended my retreat, she thought she was a happy person looking to stay that way. However, as she examined her life more closely, she could see that the choices she had been making hadn't been making her happy at all. The problem wasn't in the morality of her relationship with Matt, it was in the inequality of it.

Tamara decided to end things with Matt. Although she still wasn't sure if she wanted to be in a serious relationship, she knew any romantic entanglement she did have needed to be between two people who treated each other with equal respect.

As a consenting adult, you are free to do what ever you want with whomever you want as long as the person you are doing it with is consenting too, but it's important to make sure that you are both consenting to the same thing. I see a lot of women (and some men) damage their self-esteem by deluding themselves that their relationship is something that it isn't or by seeking to boost their confidence through the affections of others.

The only way to have healthy relationships in every aspect of your life is to value yourself, and the only way you can value yourself is if you know what is special, unique or desirable about you. You need to know what your good qualities are and why you are worth having around.

As one of my favourite actresses, Jennifer Aniston, told *Glamour*: 'Once you figure out who you are and what you love about yourself, I think it all kinda falls into place.'

Don't wait for someone else to make you feel worthwhile. Don't look for someone to 'complete' you or wait for your children to love you. Don't hold on hoping that someone who has denied you affection will finally come around or that someone who has withdrawn their love will return it. Fall in love with yourself and watch all of your other relationships blossom.

Fall in love with yourself; it's the best relationship you will ever have.

When you truly love yourself, your confidence and self-esteem will become robust enough to withstand the ups and downs of life. You will become resilient enough to maintain your self-belief regardless of the circumstances and you will feel good about who you are and the life you live, all day, every day.

The **Eighth Promise** is all about making yourself a priority in your life. Treat yourself with as much love and respect as you do the other important people in your life and make the commitment to *love yourself,* unconditionally.

Keeping the Pact

*Applying the **Eight Promises** to your life*

I hope you've found *The Kindness Pact* to be an exciting and inspiring discovery. Perhaps on some level it has been liberating to realise that your self-belief does not come from what you've got or what you've done, but the way that you treat yourself, and that knowing this releases you from the expectation that your confidence will come *one day* and allows you to feel good about yourself *today*.

Don't let this book get dusty. Keep it close by and know that if ever you are feeling insecure, vulnerable or unsure of yourself, the remedy lies in one of the **Eight Promises**.

If you would like to learn more about *The Kindness Pact* and how to keep the **Eight Promises**, visit domoniquebertolucci.com where you can download and work through *The Kindness Pact Workbook* and get free video training on how to get the life you want and love the life you've got.

Reading this book is just the beginning. It's now time to make your commitments to yourself. When you make *The Kindness Pact*, you promise to:

- stop trying to be perfect and accept yourself for who you are, as you are
- recognise that not only is your best good enough, you are good enough
- give up comparing yourself to people you know, people you used to know and people you've never met
- expect good things to come your way and stop worrying about the few occasions when they won't
- become your own best friend and only ever speak to yourself in an encouraging and supportive way
- stop saying 'I can't' and instead step outside of your comfort zone regularly
- take responsibility for who you are and what you want from life

- love yourself and make building and maintaining your confidence and self-esteem a high priority in your life.

Most importantly, by keeping the **Eight Promises**, you will finally know how to treat yourself with the same kindness, love and respect that you show the other important people in your life.

I wish you every success in maintaining the **Eight Promises** and I'd love to find out what impact they have had on your life. You can let me know at facebook.com/domoniquebertolucci.

*You deserve to feel good about who **you are** and the life **you live**.*

Acknowledgements

My first thanks, as always, go to my wonderful agent, Tara Wynne at Curtis Brown, for her never-ending belief in my work. Thank you to Fran Berry, Rihana Ries, Allison Hiew, Olivia Fleetwood and all the team at Hardie Grant for once again being such a delight to work with.

To my readers who connect with me on my Facebook page, thank you for sharing your experiences or simply stopping by to say hello. Hearing from you always makes my day.

To all my clients, past and present, the inspiring people who attend my workshops and those who buy my online programs, thank you. I love my work and it is in no small part because I get to share it with you. Thank you to Dani Magestro for making these courses and programs run so smoothly.

In this book I write about treating yourself like your best friend would and I am blessed to know firsthand how unconditional this love should be. Thank you to Alecia Benzie for being an inspiration in so many ways, Tristan Stein for believing in my hopes and dreams as much as I do, Brooke Alexander for sharing so many of the steps along the way and Lisa Willis for being the sister I always wanted.

To Marina Samen, Adele Williamson, Sarah Ashe, Samantha Gloede, Tamy Starr, Kate Forster, Mary Lusted and all my other girlfriends scattered around the world, thank you for proving that time and distance have no impact on true friendship. And to Polly Fox, thank you for your love and friendship – I wrote every chapter for you.

A never-ending thank you to my mum and dad who never failed to love me unconditionally and taught me so much about kindness along the way.

To my darling Sophia and precious Toby, thank you for bringing so much love and laughter into my life. And to Paul, for everything, always.

In loving memory of Elia Bertolucci
1921–2014

About the Author

Domonique Bertolucci is the best-selling author of *The Happiness Code: 10 keys to being the best you can be*, and the closely guarded secret behind some of the country's most successful people.

Passionate about getting the life you want *and* loving the life you've got, Domonique has a client list that reads like a who's who of CEOs and business identities, award-winning entrepreneurs and celebrities, and her workshops and online courses are attended by people from all walks of life, from all around the world.

Domonique helps her clients define their personal happiness prescription and then shows them exactly how to make it their reality.

Since writing her first book, *Your Best Life*, in 2006, Domonique has become Australia's most popular life strategist and happiness coach. More than ten million people have seen, read or heard her advice.

Domonique lives in Sydney, but her reach is truly global. In addition to her Australian clients, she has coached people in London, Amsterdam, Paris, New York, Toronto, Singapore and Hong Kong. Her weekly newsletter *Love Your Life* has readers in more than sixty countries.

When she is not working, Domonique's favourite ways to spend her time are with her husband and two children, reading a good book, and keeping up the great Italian tradition of feeding the people that you love.

Keep in touch with Domonique at:
domoniquebertolucci.com
facebook.com/domoniquebertolucci
twitter.com/fromDomonique

Find out about her courses and workshops:
domoniquebertolucci.com/you-me
howtobehappyseries.com
bbbmonline.com

Other Books by Domonique

The Happiness Code: 10 keys to being the best you can be

Love Your Life: 100 ways to start living the life you deserve

100 Days Happier: Daily inspiration for life-long happiness

Less is More: 101 ways to simplify your life